HIGHWAY 25
in the
CAROLINAS

HIGHWAY 25
in the
CAROLINAS

A Brief History

ANNE PEDEN AND JIM SCOTT

THE
History
PRESS

Published by The History Press
Charleston, SC
www.historypress.com

Images are from the collection of Anne Peden unless otherwise noted.

First published 2021

Manufactured in the United States

ISBN 9781467148092

Library of Congress Control Number: 2020948442

Notice: The information in this book is true and complete to the best of our knowledge. It is offered without guarantee on the part of the authors or The History Press. The authors and The History Press disclaim all liability in connection with the use of this book.

The old families have scattered to the winds, but the road abides with its sweet and precious memories, and the dust of our progenitors sleeps in the church yards where they worshipped.
—J.W. Daniel, Southern Christian Advocate, *1921*

As pavement would soon cover the dirt trail, J.W. Daniel reflected on the ancient road between the Saluda and Reedy Rivers from Greenville to Ninety Six, South Carolina.

To all the feet that have traveled this trace, path, wagon road, stage road and paved interstate highway since time immemorial and to the visitors who will ride it in the future. May the Road to Augusta forever be a connection to life and history and a pathway to new experiences in the Western Carolinas.

I dedicate this text to all the historians in southern Greenville County in the Fork Shoals Historical Society, the Piedmont Historic Preservation Society and the Greenville County Historic Preservation Commission who continue to record our history. To Mann Batson, whose writings challenged me; to Penny Forrester, who has taught me real research; to the Campbell clan, who make my way easier; and especially to my family, Sarah, Margie and Sims Adams, and my late husband, Raymond, who have all pushed me to keep working.
—Anne Peden

This book is dedicated to my grandmother Mary "Mae" Etta McCuen Scott. She taught me to read and remember Bible verses and local history at an early age. She told me many old stories about her childhood and even the ones her parents told her about the War Between the States and the terrible Reconstruction years. She told me all about the old plantations in the area and our relationships to those families. She told me all about Ireland and the tales of my great-grandfather on his voyage and adventures in the Great Struggle. She was my inspiration to study history and genealogy.

Also, I would like to mention all of my friends and associates of the Fork Shoals Historical Society and the Laurens County Genealogy Chapter.
—Jim Scott

CONTENTS

Acknowledgements 11
Prologue 13
Background Information 15

PART I. CONJURING THE ROAD
Chapter 1. Early Travel to Augusta: From Trace to Path to Trail 21
Chapter 2. The Dirt Trail: Opening the Backcountry
      to Road Builders 33
Chapter 3. Growth along the Road: The Coming of Mules,
      Conestogas and Stages 54
Chapter 4. Adversity: Preparing the Way 71

PART II. PAVING THE WAY
Chapter 5. Good Roads: The Push, the People and the Politics 79
Chapter 6. The Dixie Highway: A Plan to Bring Prosperity to All 86
Chapter 7. Paving the Road Politics: The Issues 93
Chapter 8. Actually Paving the Road 105
Chapter 9. The New Modern South:
      The Eisenhower Connection 110

PART III. FOR YOUR TRAVELS
Chapter 10. On the Road Again: The Dirt and the Concrete 119

CONTENTS

Chapter 11. Stories of the Road: Stories, Recollections
   and Sagas   151
 Dan's Place   151
 Cousin Tempie   152
 Cousin Dave   154
 Joe McCullough Comes to the Road   159
 Meeting Street Feud   166
 Ware Place Crossroads   168
 The Kingdom of Happy Land   171
 Hot Springs and Jewel Hill   173

Notes   175
Index   185
About the Authors   191

ACKNOWLEDGEMENTS

This work has been supported by many historians along the Augusta/ Buncombe Road. Historians and friends have given us pieces of their knowledge of local roads and stories, without which this text would not exist. Thanks to George Estes, Penny Forrester, Bettis Rainsford and Bob Dicey for their deep love of local history and for their great dedication to research and to recording the stories. Thanks to George Estes for touring us around and pointing out the ancient road beds between Princeton and Greenwood, South Carolina. George is our inspiration for learning more and beginning the intense search for finding the original roads. Thanks to Bettis Rainsford for also providing us a tour and the research he has published for the Edgefield area. Thanks to Bob Dicey for his tour, research and historical records on the Greenville Army Air Base and Donaldson Air Base. Thanks to Scooter Byars for taking Jim fishing on Lake Greenwood to get photos of the Smith Bridge pillars. Thanks to Bonnie Orr for supporting us with research. Thanks to Kyle Campbell for riding along when needed, for helping us see the cuts on the terrain maps, locating the latitude and longitude, for other technology aids and for picking me up from ditches. Thanks to Barbara Adams, Cathy Morton, Bonnie and Raymond Orr and Nancy Rector for riding on searching trips and being another pair of eyes. Thanks to Charles Garrison for scanning photographs and postcards and to Penny Forrester, Cheryl MacKnight and Cathy Morton for editing text and for the great suggestions. Thanks to the folks at the South Carolina State Historic Preservation Office—particularly Brad Sauls, Virigina Harness and

Edwin Breeden—for encouraging the work and for accepting and editing a National Register application leading to the research background. Another great aid to this roadwork has been the folks at The History Press, including Hilary Parrish and Chad, whose last name is very applicable—Rhoad.

Thanks to all the great folks we met along the road who wondered what these crazy strangers were doing driving, stopping, parking and taking pictures along their roads. They were all so helpful by providing directions and verification that "yes" that is a section of the old road or "no" you need to go on down or over yonder. We were blessed to know that locals knew the stories of the road and were happy to help misguided strangers find the overgrown ruts and cuts. During times of the coronavirus, we traveled to portions of North Carolina with social distancing and found many folks very supportive by sharing stories and ruts or concrete across their properties.

Also, thanks to the many historians who wrote and published information about the ancient road early in the 1800s and the journals of travelers from the colonial period. Thanks also to the folks who travel these old roads now just to see a glimpse of what it was like once upon a time, the Dixie Highway roadies on Facebook. Thanks to twentieth-century travel writers who set the stage for experiencing a road, William Least Heat-Moon specifically. This has been an exciting journey.

Photographs from the excursions and postcards belong to the authors unless otherwise noted.

PROLOGUE

As drivers and riders in vehicles, almost all people are deeply concerned with the roads they travel throughout their lives. Riders are belted into positions of viewing the passing scenery, and drivers steer through those views, navigating the most direct paths to and from their destinations. The authors of this text have come to love a road: U.S. Highway 25 in southern Greenville County, South Carolina. Both of us have traveled the Augusta Road continually since before Eisenhower was president, and our ancestors had done so since at least the time of Andrew Jackson. Our rubber-wheeled contraptions have been over this road so much that they could almost return to the stable like our grandparents' mules would have.

Knowledge of this highway for the writers was like that of other travelers until about 2015, when we, Anne Peden and Jim Scott, began working together on a preservation project, an 1812 Federal house set up against this road near Princeton, South Carolina. The history of the Joseph McCullough House or Cedarhurst is long and meaningful and pulled us into its story. Cedarhurst was a thriving plantation during the nineteenth century, but it was also an inn, stagecoach stop, post office and entertainment venue with horse racing, an occasional circus and a ballroom situated on the main road—a road much older than the house itself.

In the process of studying Cedarhurst, the story of the road became prominent when a fellow historian, George Estes, led us to wagon road ruts near McCullough's, and we set off on the search for ruts and ditches. Spending over a year retracing the now wooded wagon road led us to the

A deep cut from the early drover and stage road can be seen above the current dirt road on Old Stage Road west of Edgefield.

concrete remains denoting old United States Highway 25. Forging into an understanding of the importance of the road to the growth of the backcountry pushed us to share and promote the road as well as Cedarhurst by applying for a National Register designation for the historic road and by publishing this text. So, our story starts along a bison trace during the time of the Carolina colonies and ends in the first half of the twentieth century, when this historic trade path evolved into a nationally known interstate, the Dixie Highway, and finally, United States Highway 25. Because of our personal histories with this important road, please understand if this work leans to the Upstate and southern Greenville County, South Carolina.

BACKGROUND INFORMATION

U nited States Highway 25 traverses the western part of both Carolina states along a north to south path approximately along the 82nd longitude line from north of Hot Springs, North Carolina, to the Savannah River at North Augusta, South Carolina. It can be documented to at least 1766–68.

Miss Sue Scott wrote of the road in her 1961 history of the Scott and McCullough families of southern Greenville County, South Carolina. These farming families had lived along the road for over one hundred years, and in the first paragraph of the text, she made it clear that she would refer to the road as the Augusta Road. Although she did allow that it went from Michigan to Miami, she never used any other moniker. She had seen the changes to the road in her lifetime. She had watched the Lowcountry carriages coming up to the mountains and the drovers' herds passing down to the Savannah River. Obviously, she understood the significance of the ports at Augusta to this historic highway through the Carolinas. In this history of the road, we, too, will use the appropriate names that apply to the various sections of the Buncombe Turnpike, Saluda Gap and Augusta Road, as well as other specific names currently applied to the approximately 225-mile historic road through North and South Carolina.

This road was an ancient path used by animals and Natives to negotiate the Kentucky grasslands through Tennessee, the mountains of North Carolina and South Carolina to the navigable parts of the Savannah River at Augusta, Georgia, in order to reach the Atlantic Ocean between South

Carolina and Savannah, Georgia. The old dirt path became a trading path with the Cherokee, a wagon road in the 1800s and a concrete paved road just after the turn of the twentieth century. As automobile numbers grew, weather-resistant roads became more important, and the road trip became popular in the 1910s. The Dixie Highway was designed to lure northerners from as far as Sault Ste. Marie, Michigan, on the Canadian border, through the sunny southland to the paradise of Miami, Florida. The Carolina portion of the Eastern Division was designated in 1918, and the Dixie Highway became an important byway for tourists through the Carolinas. The federal government set up the numbered interstate highway system in 1926, changing the name to U.S. Highway 25. Actual paving of some sections of the new concrete road was not completed until 1931. The name Dixie Highway was relatively short-lived, but the impact of the road and U.S. 25 has lasted. The centennial of the creation of U.S. 25 is soon coming and the Dixie Highway's centennial is ongoing through 2031, the date of the completion of paving in the Carolinas.

Six key components of our roads—initially water and geography and, later, commerce, military, travel and industry—were regulated by the government in some manner. Early in the history of the Carolinas, Lowcountry wealthy plantation owners and merchants around Charleston, South Carolina, influenced backcountry and mountain life and, therefore, roads from the very beginning of the colonies. The several cultures along the road often clashed, but the ability to make a living from the new resources available moved up from the coast to the mountains. The Lowcountry cultures included wealthy plantation owners and their families, merchants, enslaved peoples, traders, craftsmen, store owners, educators and clergy. Native Americans present worked to form alliances for trade with all the colonists.

The South Carolina backcountry culture was composed mostly of subsistence farming initially and later larger plantations with varying numbers of Africans as enslaved workers. Some educated clergy developed small congregations and traveled to brush arbors or parlors, staying in preacher rooms of homes along the way, and led in the establishment of schools. Also, a small number of accomplished men were searching for various resources that had been identified in the backcountry, such as the clays found along the fall line marking the ancient sea level. Others searched for gold. Businesses developed in pottery, lumber and livestock. The Appalachian mountain culture was almost totally subsistence farming in the valleys plus moonshine making along the creeks well into the twentieth century. War and military groups affected the roads time and again as well. And as always, funding the creation and upkeep of roads was a challenge, pulling small and large government oversight into the mix.

Over time, necessities for human and animal travel began to be met, bringing along the lodging and food establishments. Various types of support were provided for the different classes, all aimed at being profitable. Commerce was the main reason for building roads, and money was needed for ongoing upkeep as well as for support of those traveling the backcountry. Money drove the use, construction and maintenance of roads then as it does now.

For hundreds of years, historians have depended on travel writers to provide insights into the lives and places of those who went before us. One clergyman of note who repeatedly moved along the early path was Bishop Francis Asbury of the Methodist Episcopal Church. Asbury dedicated his life to spreading the words of Jesus in the colonies and journaling as he went. Around the turn of the 1800s, he ministered along the byway that became the United States Highway 25. His wisdom from over two hundred years ago still applies to the road today: "I cannot record great things of religion in this quarter; *but cotton sells high*. I fear there is more gold than grace."[1]

PART I

CONJURING THE ROAD

Old Stage Road outside Edgefield, South Carolina, was an ancient path and is still a public dirt road.

Chapter 1

EARLY TRAVEL TO AUGUSTA

From Trace to Path to Trail

When the colonists reached the New World, there were already paths crisscrossing the land. These passageways were formed by animals and the Natives long living here. No horses or beasts of burden were known in the forests and meadows to the original peoples. Native Americans were their own burden carriers. Proficient in crafting baskets and sledges, they moved what was needed. As time passed and their world was invaded by Europeans, they received horses in trade, and their walking paths became pack train trails and later wagon roads. Trade led to most of these changes.

Early travel writing provides records of the backcountry of North and South Carolina in pre-colonial and colonial times dating to the travels of Spaniards Hernando de Soto and Juan Pardo in the 1500s and of English captain George Chicken coming from Charles Town and William Byrd surveying the line between North Carolina and Virginia in the early 1700s. These records support the early use of the animal and Indian trails already available and describe the geography and natives of the Carolinas during some of the earliest visits by Europeans. Early records are documentation of travel for governmental purposes and, because of this, are accessible to future generations, whereas most civilian descriptions of travels were private letters unless completed by scientists for publication

Buffalo drawing from a French map of America, 1690, by Licues Francoises.

A 1690 French map of Virginia, Carolina and the eastern parts of what would later be Tennessee and Georgia.

such as *The Travels of William Bartram*, who was a naturalist, or John J. Audubon's *The Birds of America*, both of whom traveled in the Carolinas. After the Revolution, historians published accounts using many documents and interviews, providing more concise and understandable histories. These works afford insight into the beginnings of travel and roads in the Carolinas.

The Traces: Bison

Great numbers of animals roved the eastern woodlands and the high meadows in the southlands when the Europeans came to the Carolinas. Bison, elk, wolf, wildcat, turkey and deer, not to mention vast numbers of black bear, coursed the uplands where forests, prairies and great canebrakes supplied their various needs. The stately old-growth timberland trees were dispersed enough for grasses to cover the floor of the forests and for deer and buffalo to be seen among the trees at great distances.[2]

The largest and most prolific of the path builders in the southern colonies were the great herds of buffalo that natives across North America called *yanasa*, the bull of god.[3] Eastern bison were smaller than plains buffalo but probably of the same genetic stock,[4] although some classify them as an eastern wood bison, related to the Canadian species.[5] Great throngs of these buffalo were recorded near Nashville and the surrounding salt licks in the mid-1700s. The French Broad River Valley in North Carolina was a well-known hunting ground, as the animals were funneled between the water and the rocky mountainsides.[6] Instinctively, animals chose to travel the most level and shortest passages through the lowest and richest gaps in this mountainous terrain[7] leading to Asheville, where two main buffalo traces and Indian paths crossed at what is now called Pack Square in downtown. The French Broad trail later became part of the Carolina U.S. Highway 25 leading into North and South Carolina.[8]

On into South Carolina even into the mid-state region at the fall line where ocean waves once lapped, buffalo were recorded in great numbers when settlers first came from Virginia and Pennsylvania. One early settler counted one hundred grazing on a single acre of ground in the Edgefield and Abbeville area. Another pioneer stated, "Their deep worn trails leading to favorite ranges and licks, marked the country in every direction, and long after the struggling settlement had become a flourishing community, and not a buffalo remained in those parts, these paths could still be traced along the

Buffalo grazing in a savannah.

creek and its tributaries." William Bartram passed through old Fort Charlotte on the Savannah River while traveling to the lower Cherokee towns in 1773. He described a spot just north of the fort where great numbers of moss-covered bones of men and buffaloes were scattered.[9] The last of these great roaming beasts was killed in North Carolina near Asheville on Bull Creek in 1799, and they were extinct by 1825.[10] They are gone but not forgotten, for many roads and some sites still carry their remembrances: Buffalo, South Carolina, near Union; Old Buffalo Church Road, Blacksburg, South Carolina; Old Buffalo Ford Road, Asheboro, North Carolina; Bison Court near Charlotte, North Carolina; Old Trace Road, Concord, North Carolina; Lick Branch, New Gilead, North Carolina; and Lickville Presbyterian Church, Pelzer, South Carolina, which is on the Augusta Road in southern Greenville County.

THE PATHS: NATIVES AND TRADERS

It is probable that the Native Americans developed their trading paths across the Carolinas following the buffalo traces.[11] In this mountainous region of the southern Appalachians, the main tribe was the Cherokee, and in the farther reaches of the states, east toward the sea, the Catawba tribe ruled. Many of the creek and road names relating to bison are in the domain of the Catawba. These tribes shared hunting grounds in Upstate South Carolina in the area of southern Greenville County.[12] But the Great Cherokee Path was the main footpath leading from Charles Town to the lower Cherokee towns in the northwestern South Carolina colony.[13] On early deeds and plats, it was listed as Old Keowee Road,[14] and the path continued to the Over Hill villages[15] in Tennessee. South Carolinians designated the Cherokee lands as the Nation, and part of Nation Road near Ware Shoals, South Carolina, led to the Cherokee Nation's lower towns in Upstate South Carolina and was a section of the dirt road to Augusta.[16]

Three Cherokee settlements dominated the southern Appalachian Mountains: the Overhill Towns of Tennessee included Chota, the major settlement, and Tanasi, for which the state was named; the Out, Middle and Valley Towns were in the mountains of North Carolina and included the current Cherokee Indian Reservation; and the Lower Towns included Keowee and Toxaway in South Carolina's Pickens and Oconee Counties and some areas of northern Georgia.[17] Several South Carolina sites were named by traders for their distance from Keowee Town, such as Six Mile, the creek and town; Twelve Mile Creek; and Ninety Six at the Revolutionary War Star Fort. Numerous place names can be noted across western North Carolina, such as Cherokee Drive, Road or Trail. Along the lands of these three settlements, some of their trails later became parts of U.S. Highway 25 in the Carolinas.

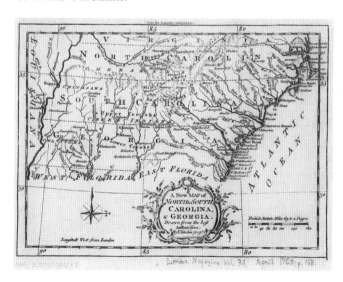

"A New Map of North & South Carolina, & Georgia. Drawn from the Best Authorities, by T. Kitchin Greg," circa 1700s. Note the extended lines of these three states reaching the Mississippi River. *Wikimedia Commons.*

Only moving in single file, the Cherokee traders wore the path to a depth of ten feet or more in some areas and left a ditch for later historians to find.[18] When available, ridges provided the easiest travel by avoiding fording creeks and repetitive hills.[19] The valley road north of Asheville along the French Broad River from Tennessee turned into a ridge road in South Carolina—a ridge between the Saluda and Reedy Rivers, both initiating in northern Greenville County. The ridge continued nearly to the star fort at Ninety Six, and then the path split into four: the road to Charles Town, Island Ford Road to the town of Saluda, the road to Long Canes and Martin Town Road,[20] sometimes called the road to Savannah Town,[21] and traveling through the fall line.

These paths to Charles Town and Old Savannah Town were the major trade routes for the Cherokee hunters bringing pelts and native slaves from warring tribes to the white men for sale. This lucrative slave trade began only four years after the creation of Charles Town. Although against the statutes of the colonies, the trade in indigenous slaves continued unabated until after the Revolution, but in the meantime, the African slave trade had followed suit.[22]

Pelts were the next most important trade products for the Cherokee since animals were plentiful across their lands. By 1707, Charles Town was trading possibly one thousand miles to the west, and many colonists had become traders with the Cherokee and other nations to the southwest. Some of these men had lived among the Natives for decades, marrying native women and raising families.[23] They attempted to marry daughters of chiefs to insert themselves into the dynasty of the culture. Some sent their offspring to be educated in the Charles Town schools providing tribal leadership, and with the ability to speak several languages, they could bargain with officials from Spain, England and France.[24]

Historian James H. Richardson suggested that there were two groups of Englishmen who moved into the backcountry of the Carolinas before settlers came—the Indian traders and the cattlemen—and both groups used the Cherokee for profit. The traders built trading posts near the Indian villages and exchanged guns, ammunition, rum and trinkets for furs and skins. The cow men found open meadows in the Cherokee hunting grounds for pastures where they herded cattle and horses in great numbers and built pens to tame them for the trail.[25] The town of Cowpens, in Spartanburg County, South Carolina, was named for this early cattle raising industry and later became a stop on cattle drives.[26]

Basically, during this early period, trade with the Cherokee and other nations was by individual traders and cattlemen with no oversight, but by the early 1700s, abuses of the Natives had caused complaints to the provincial government in Charles Town, and statutes were passed for their protection. By 1707, regulations were set forth for all trade with Indians, causing the colonist traders to purchase licenses and bonds to guarantee compliance to the new rules. But corruption followed and the regulations were ignored, allowing worse cruelties, even from false missionaries of the Gospel who set Native against Native for profit. As early as 1717, the Cherokee requested a garrison and trading house at Savannah Town (also called New Windsor), and the following year, a garrison was established, Fort Moore, on the South Carolina side of the Savannah River at what later became Hamburg.[27]

Around this time, historian John H. Logan described a trading day at Savannah Town after trade items arrived from Charles Town:[28]

> *On their outskirts were encamped numerous caravans of pack-trains, with their roistering drivers, who are mostly mischievous boys. The smoke from a hundred camp-fires curl above the thick tops of the trees, and the woods resound with the neighing of horses, and the barking and howling of hungry Indian dogs. A large supply of goods has arrived from Charleston, and every pack-saddle came down from the Nation loaded with skins and furs, and these being now displayed to the best advantage, the work of barter begins.*
>
> *In the open air and in the trading-house are congregated a motley assembly of pack-horsemen, traders, hunters, squaws, children, soldiers, and stately Indian warriors—some silent and grave, seemingly uninterested in the scene; but the greater number loudly huckstering, and obstinately contending over their respective commodities in trade, in many barbarous tongues.*[29]

From this, one can imagine the raucous trading day, but hunters left with powder and ball, squaws found the perfect bright-colored fabric for a new dress and warriors acquired updated guns and ammunition. This scene was lively, but trading abuses and other atrocities continued.[30]

Around the beginning of the eighteenth century, Indian trade was the most lucrative business in the Carolinas. Each Cherokee town had at least one trading post doing significant business in deer, buffalo and bear skins provided by the hunters. The traders even organized the braves into camps provided with guns and munitions. The posts would permit credit during the summers when no hunting was allowed, causing the Indians to be tied

A drawing of Native Americans with American animals from the French map of America, 1690.

to the trader to repay debts the next season. For the Cherokee, it became a vicious cycle.[31]

As this trade began to fall off somewhat, Sir Alexander Cummings set out from England in 1730 and met with Cherokee chieftains, sealing a treaty of basically friendship, which continued the same rights of the white man in Cherokee country. From this meeting, six of the chiefs, including well-known Atta Kulla Kulla, took a voyage to London, where they were treated royally. By 1731, when peltry trade began to decline, 225,000 deer skins alone made their way to Charles Town.[32] In 1746 at Ninety Six, another meeting was held with the great chief Old Hop, and the royal governor came, traveling with four companies of troops and many gentlemen. This stately group was attempting to prevent the French from influencing the Cherokee Nation.[33] In 1755, when the game of the backcountry was greatly depleted, 25,000 skins were still brought down for trade.[34]

Over time, English traders were less and less trustworthy, and by 1750, thieving and general lawlessness in the backcountry was rampant. With Charles Town two hundred miles away, outlaws dominated and traveled throughout, stealing horses from cattlemen and robbing the pack trains. Finally, in 1753, a formal treaty with the Cherokee gave Carolinians the right to construct forts within the Nation, and with Fort Prince George opening in 1755, conditions improved somewhat. The French and Indian War in the northern states in 1754 began a new migration of settlers to the South. Pioneers traveled down the Great Wagon Road from Pennsylvania and Virginia into the open areas of the Carolinas.[35] But the Indian War with the Cherokee came about soon thereafter. It was caused by continued abuses, trade in rum and smallpox brought to the Nation on a pack train of goods. This strife caused the new settlers great hardships doled out by Native raiding parties.[36] After the Cherokee war, the Carolinas were on the precipice of a new era of growth, but mixed loyalties were prevalent through the Revolution, provoking battles among families, neighbors and Natives.

THE TRAILS: PACK TRAINS, DROVERS, WAGONS

As Indian trade developed and their paths grew deep from pack trains carrying pelts and cattle herds coming to market, the paths widened and became trails for the passage of wagons and larger herds. Already living in the backcountry were the English and Scotch-Irish traders, many of whom had married Cherokee princesses and established homesteads on the best waterways. After a period of relative calm, with forts being constructed along the boundaries of the Cherokee Nation, a rift was forming among Lowcountry leaders, New England colonists and England. Upstate settlers were divided on the topic of freeing the colonies—basically depending on their individual situations relating to commerce and taxation.

Pioneers came south along the Great Wagon Road or up from Charles Town, acquiring land grants from the king of England and settling in

Calves in a Woodland, by Carleton Wiggins, 1886.

Ninety Six, Laurens or Spartanburg Districts. After the Revolution, the grants came as payment for services rendered. These settlers cut trees, built cabins and began farming along with hunting. After the Revolution, folks in the backcountry of both North and South Carolina were invested not only in establishing more trade and commerce for their products but also in forming local, state and national governments for their protection against thieves and Cherokee raids.

When Augusta was established in 1736, much trade was drawn off from Fort Moore, and Savannah Town became isolated and essentially unused.

Augusta grew prolifically and was the center of trade there until the town of Hamburg was built on the South Carolina side of the river in the following century.[37] Opening up the Cherokee-held lands in the Carolinas increased traffic on the dirt road to Augusta, and a ferry over the Savannah River was established there about 1747 near Fort Moore on the South Carolina side across from Augusta.[38] Ferries and some bridges were assigned to the builders as early profit-making ventures where they were allowed to charge tolls for crossing.

Ninety Six District covered the whole of western South Carolina and was made the courthouse town for the backcountry in 1769. A licensed Indian trader, Robert Goudy, may have been the first permanent settler at Ninety Six about 1737. Later, he purchased land and built a store, house and barn. Rum was a major commodity. In 1759, a stockade was built around his barn by Governor Lyttelton's company; it became known as Goudy's Fort or Fort Ninety Six. The first Revolutionary battle in South Carolina took place there in November 1775, and the Loyalist Star Fort, now a national monument, survived a siege by the Patriots in 1781.[39]

The name Ninety Six was changed to Cambridge in 1787, and the village was known for a literary association and a college. Cambridge was a site on the trade trail, with four taverns and inns providing accommodations and food on the road to Augusta. Traders came down from the mountain a couple of times a year. They brought wagonloads of chestnuts, cabbages, venison, hams and tobacco, as well as a supply of "the critter"—homemade corn whiskey. But an epidemic in 1815–1816 began to cause these folk to pass Cambridge by.[40] A ledger was found for one of the last stores in Cambridge, and some items purchased were: candles; raisins, twenty-five cents per pound; cheese, twenty cents per pound; cigars by "the bunch"; whiskey, one dollar per gallon; rum and gin, one dollar per gallon; peach brandy and rose cordial, thirty-seven cents per quart; and a "box of Lucifers" (friction matches invented in 1829), twenty-five cents per box.[41] The old Cambridge title reverted back to Ninety Six in the late 1800s.

In the same year Ninety Six acquired the courthouse, Daniel Boone was traveling on hunting trails across North Carolina into Tennessee and Kentucky to search out this Wild West.[42] Boone's first trip into Tennessee in 1769 was probably by the most direct route through upstate North Carolina, exiting at Zionsville into the Tennessee mountains with a small pack train carrying camping equipment, salt, ammunitions and other supplies.[43]

North of Ninety Six along the Saluda River (often found written *Saludy* in some early documents and probably pronounced accordingly as well),[44] early traders had moved into the eastern hunting lands of the Nation in South Carolina well before the Revolution commenced in the backcountry, and small settlements had already been working farms. Also well known in South Carolina's backcountry on the eastern part of the Nation was the homestead of Richard Pearis on the falls of the Reedy River in what was then called Great Plains, now downtown Greenville. Other settlers were probably grouped in widely dispersed communities like Golden Grove on Grove Creek southwest of Pearis, where Alexander Cameron kept "cow pens" near the Saluda River, and in the northeast corner, several families developed the area around Gowensville (later known as the Dark Corner). Both of these sites were on the dirt road from Augusta to Buncombe County, North Carolina. Some pioneers were probably spread out across the county though, and one piece of evidence was that "public" roads crisscrossed in all directions.[45]

One of these "public" roads went from Pearis's homestead on the Reedy to Ninety Six and on to Augusta. This information identifies the trade road south to Augusta, Georgia, at least to the arrival of Pearis in the county between 1766 and 1768[46]—over 250 years of documented existence in the backcountry through the Cherokee Nation. The port of Savannah Town on the Savannah River was the closest navigable river to the sea from eastern Kentucky and Tennessee, and Natives across the Southeast had used the Augusta site for hundreds, maybe thousands, of years. (Numerous archaeological sites dating back at least three thousand years have been documented on both sides of the Savannah River near Augusta.)[47]

Early pioneers spent much time, effort and money traveling and eventually building a better road system than the traces and paths they found on arrival in the Carolinas. The passages they built can still be found in the wooded areas of the old Buncombe Turnpike and the old road to Augusta if passersby slow down to travel existing public dirt roads and look carefully for deep and wide ditches in the roadside shadows.

Chapter 2

THE DIRT TRAIL

Opening the Backcountry to Road Builders

Opening the western Carolinas after the Revolution meant taking control of the Cherokee Nation and dominating the Natives. As the states and the Union expanded across the continent, the belief in the right to own the land grew. The Lowcountry in South Carolina continued to dominate the culture and government. That dominance followed the Augusta/Buncombe Road up to at least the Tennessee line and somewhat into the stock pens of Kentucky.[48] The plantation owners grew their wealth, and they brought the money with them when they bought land and built summer homes along the road. The livestock trade burgeoned coming down the Buncombe Road and later Buncombe Turnpike to the Saluda Gap to Augusta. Then the movement of people and animals brought commerce along the way and profits for the local farmers, innkeepers, tavern owners and stock camps.

As cotton became a lucrative commodity, its production in the western part of South Carolina furthered the growth of plantations as well as the beginnings of the cotton industry. In the backcountry, when the War Between the States approached, many families were divided on the issue again, as they had been during the Revolution, especially those living on the Tennessee and North Carolina borders.[49] The antebellum years were prosperous for the dominant class but often at the expense of others.

Governance and enterprise filled this early period in the life of the young nation. It also was a time of expansion, pushing toward the west. It was the right time for a road in the western Carolinas.

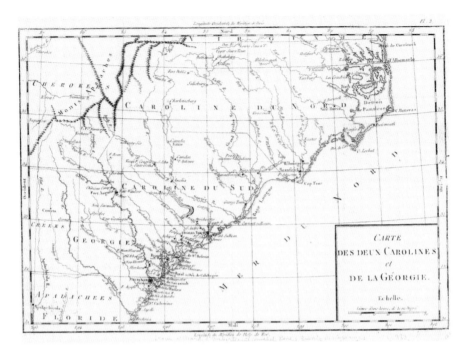

Map of the Two Carolinas and of the Georgia, by Echelle. *Digital History,* digitalhistory.uh.edu.

OPENING THE BACKCOUNTRY

In South Carolina a treaty was made with the Cherokee Nation in 1777 at DeWitts Corner, now Due West, on the border of the Nation. This treaty acquired the Cherokee lands in northwestern South Carolina for the state, but the agreement was basically shelved until the end of the Revolution in 1783. Called the Washington District, the old Indian Territory included current Greenville, Anderson, Pickens and Oconee Counties. The Lower Cherokee villages disappeared. When the state moved forward with the actual acquisition of the Cherokee lands, the traders already residing there were displaced as the state looked to use those properties to repay debts. For the Revolutionary War soldiers, lands in the Nation were deeded out as compensation, and settlers moved in legally. Greenville County was officially a county in 1786. On the North and South Carolina borderlands with Georgia and Tennessee, French and English influences continued into the 1800s.[50]

In North Carolina, much wrangling ensued after the Revolution. There was the issue of the extended lands to the west all the way to the

Mississippi and the Natives living here, and there was even a period when a new state of Franklin was considered. Sadly, many peaceful Cherokee were slaughtered during this period, and many were pushed farther toward Tennessee and the Over Hill villages. As in South Carolina, the Wild West was here in the backcountry. After boundary lines were drawn between Tennessee and North Carolina and Buncombe County was formed in 1791, the territory covered the whole area from Rutherford County westward. Little governance was provided until into the 1800s.[51] During the period between 1808 and 1925, county lines affecting Buncombe changed several times,[52] and by about 1833, Indian lands had been confiscated, moving most Cherokee to Oklahoma.[53]

Trade continued through this transition period. Although already greatly depleted, pelts and skins were still traded, slaves were bought and sold, minerals were mined, forests were turned into fields of cotton and tobacco and roads were improved as pioneers moved in to settle the West. Lowcountry planters had begun to visit the "Mountain Town" of Greenville and also Flat Rock, North Carolina, just over the Saluda Gap, and then they followed the trade trails farther north.

ROAD BUILDERS

Pioneers came into the Piedmont and mountains of the Carolinas in covered wagons, bringing their families, animals and some household goods. After a few years of hard work creating farms and communities, these early settlers were ready to make their homes permanent. Communities built along water sources grew, and roads from place to place began to need to accommodate those wagons as never before. The North Carolina and South Carolina mountains presented special struggles to all, especially travelers and road builders.

Daniel Boone's trip across the Blue Ridge on horseback was not like maneuvering a wagon up the French Broad River Valley surrounded by steep mountain sides. In fact, Colonel J. Barnett was the first to accomplish a wagon trip there in about 1785. By mounting two big wheels on the lower side and pulling and pushing and sometimes just literally picking up the wagon completely, he opened a business, charging five dollars when successful.[54] Mountain men attempting to construct a road may have followed the process similar to the buffalo setting trails. A steer or hog would be taken to the lowest gap in the area, and then farmers would drive the animal up through the gap, marking the path along the way.[55]

Historian John Arthur concludes that during 1795, after assessing several possible routes for wagons to pass over the Appalachians, the first wagon passed from Tennessee into North Carolina, crossing over the Paint Mountain to Hot Springs (then Warm Springs). He also suggests that it must be the road Bishop Asbury traveled several times in the very early 1800s. The bishop passed through the Paint Mountains, providing a timeline of road improvements.

First, in November 1800, Asbury crossed the Nolichucky River in Tennessee, stopping at Major Gragg's eighteen miles below the river ferry. Just past the Paint Rock (covered with ancient Native petroglyphs), a horse and chaise got upset, and when Asbury turned to see, the poor roan and the load were wedged against a sapling, just saving them from the river. They reached Warm Springs following the French Broad later in the day.[56] Then in 1802, Asbury required the aid of a pine sapling to work his way down the steepest and roughest parts of Paint Mountain. He was able to find room and board below Warm Springs with William Neilson and thirty other travelers who had "dropped in."[57] Finally, in October 1803, as he traversed Paint Mountain once again, he was passing through a newly worked gap, making the road down Paint Creek much more to his liking.[58] Other evidence suggests that Philip Hoodenpile had been charged with the upkeep of a road from Warm Springs to Newport, Tennessee, which was completed by 1812.[59]

Mountain road builders encountered many obstacles. They followed the path of least resistance by following the steer or hog up the gap to find the easiest way. Two geographic structures were well suited for travel, a valley or a ridge, but there were issues with both. The valley along a creek or river was the easiest to build but was prone to flooding and cliffs approaching the edge of the waterway. Sometimes the cliff would force fording to the opposite side or taking a gap along a stream to its headwaters, going over the cliff and then returning to the valley road. Another possibility was trying to go over the obstacle—a steep climb. Ridges usually offered fewer trees and were more level along the top, as well as being wider for wagon passage, but the mountain ridges were usually too steep for the livestock to conquer. The builders usually avoided ledges and cliffs, going as far around them as necessary through the woods. At times when forced to attack the rocky cliffs, pioneer builders used gunpowder and fire to crack the surface of rocks in order to begin excavations.[60] All of these tactics were probably used along the French Broad River from the Tennessee line to Asheville prior to 1830.

CONESTOGA

As the wagon road from Kentucky and Tennessee developed, it brought more trade in Conestoga covered wagons and droves of livestock changing South Carolina's Upstate forever. Recognizing the prospect of wealth entering the state through the Saluda Gap, the state legislature moved to improve the road. The first known wagon passing through the Saluda Gap on the South Carolina line was probably on the road Colonel Elias Earle and John William Gowan opened for $4,000 in 1793.[61] By 1802, Governor John Drayton felt that opening up the road had provided a new source of wealth for the state, allowing the General Assembly to plan an even better road up the mountain.

Right: Eastern Conestoga wagon train. *Pinterest*.

Below: Poinsett Bridge near the Old Augusta Road in northern Greenville County, South Carolina.

Designated the State Road, this road was generally understood to be a better funnel for the trade of goods and stock to Charleston (Charles Town's name was changed after the Revolution). At the site of Merritt's camp below the gap, the State Road veered to the east, bypassing all major towns except Columbia, but the road that had always been the way to Augusta forked there to the southwest toward Greenville. It became known as Buncombe Road or Augusta Road, and most drovers continued on it to the closer port at the Savannah River.[62]

This new road through the Saluda Gap was an engineering feat that was completed in just months. Engineers John Wilson and Abram Blanding guided the work and constructed a seventeen-foot-wide road narrowing to ten feet where cut through rock. Forty-four small bridges and three large arched ones were constructed of stone, with one still visible from Callahan Mountain Road off Old U.S. 25 and one moved to Cleveland Park in Greenville, South Carolina. A tollhouse was set at the foot of the mountain to waylay costs, and when it was complete, one traveler stated that the ascension difficulties were completely alleviated, and on descending, a wagon was able to pass without locking a wheel.[63]

Following the completion of the Saluda Gap Turnpike in South Carolina, North Carolina's support of the Buncombe Turnpike rose. In 1824, the legislature incorporated the turnpike "for the purpose of laying out and making a turnpike road from the Saluda Gap, in the county of Buncombe, by way of Smith's (bridge), Maryville, Asheville and Warm Springs, to the Tennessee line." By 1828, the turnpike was complete,[64] and prosperity ensued along the improved road in both Carolinas for at least one hundred years.

CAROLINA TOWNS ON THE ROAD

Basically, the Buncombe Turnpike and the Augusta Road followed two major rivers from the Tennessee line through Buncombe County across western South Carolina to the fall line—the French Broad and the Saluda. The French Broad is so named because it flowed west mostly through Tennessee's French territory in the 1700s; the Cherokee called it "racing waters."[65] It is one of a few rivers in the states that flows northwest to the Mississippi. The Saluda River was named for a tribe of Native Americans who passed through South Carolina, settling for a time and leaving the name

River of Corn. The Saluda forms in northern Greenville County from the North and South Saluda tributaries. The North Saluda leads toward Saluda Gap. From the Saluda near Ninety Six and Cambridge, two roads lead to Augusta: Martintown Road and Old Edgefield Road through the village of Meeting Street. There were three roads leaving Edgefield: Old Stage Road, Sweetwater Road and the road to the Pine House. The Savannah River dividing South Carolina and Georgia at Augusta was the major port to the sea during the early 1800s.

Villages grew up along the road to support the traffic moving down to the Savannah River or Charleston.

THROUGH THE VALLEY

The drover's road at the state line came across from Greeneville, Tennessee, at the Paint Rock, which was covered with petroglyphs, and moved up the French Broad River. Drovers and hogs and other stock quickly arrived at Warm Springs, North Carolina.

Hot Springs, North Carolina, called Warm Springs during the early 1800s, was along the French Broad River and was known for the warm healing springs in the valley there. The name changed to Hot Springs after an even warmer spring was found in the mid-1800s. Native Americans were aware of it, but the first white men were from a band of mountain riflemen seeking supplies for soldiers at the Kentucky fort at Boonesboro. They waded across the warm French Broad in 1778. William Neilson operated an inn where Bishop Francis Asbury visited at least three times at the turn of the 1800s, and by 1808, Neilson owned the lands surrounding the springs. According to Hot Springs historian Della Hazel Moore, another establishment of the time was the dangerous tavern along the drover's road (now River Road) owned by the Chunns. Many robberies and even murders were carried out here, and such happenings were prolific along the road. Traps were set into the road with a pivoting door so that when an animal stepped down on the door, it would flip the unsuspecting stock into a box or pit.[66]

In 1831, two Patton brothers from Ireland purchased the inn and springs, and over time, they improved it into a resort so that by the late 1840s, the brick hotel was frequented by a large number of fashionable and sickly people from all the southern states. Accommodating 250 patrons, there was music, dancing, bowling, bathing, riding and fishing available for entertainment.

During the War Between the States, Henry Rumbough purchased the hotel and set about caring for and running it. He also acquired the stagecoach route from Greeneville, Tennessee, to Greenville, South Carolina, down the Buncombe Turnpike, bringing many of the Lowcountry elites to his resort. South Carolinians visited here as well as New Yorkers, and South Carolina governor Wade Hampton constructed a summer home downtown. It was built with brick ballast from ships in Charleston and transported up the mountains by oxcart.[67]

After the hotel burned in 1884, Rumbough sold the property to a group of northern businessmen who built a fine new Mountain Park Hotel, but without Rumbough's personality, the hotel visitation slid, and he soon regained possession. The four-story Mountain Park contained two hundred bedrooms with marble throughout. One of the largest and finest hotels in the South, it finally closed in 1914. During World War I, it was leased to the government as a German internment camp containing nearly two thousand detainees from ships caught in U.S. ports at the beginning of the war.

The Mountain Park Hotel burned in January 1920, leaving one of the earliest and most historic of the towns along the river road without a fine establishment. Now the springs are used as a day resort, and the Appalachian Trail passes through downtown, where a large stone Dixie Highway marker greets visitors.[68] It is also a monument to the Patton sisters.

WALNUT is a very small community between Hot Springs and Marshall with a large cemetery that surrounds an early 1800s white church building. Within its walls rests a pioneer log cabin. The cabin was the original courthouse for the area once called Jewel Hill, and the cabin logs can be seen at the southeastern corner of the structure. The view is most stunning from the rear of the church across the cemetery and Blue Ridge Mountains.

MARSHALL sits between the French Broad River and mountain cliffs confined to a narrow strip of land with beautiful turn-of-the-twentieth-century buildings, many of which are in the National Register of Historic Places. Several historic markers grace the lawn at the courthouse.

WEAVERVILLE is another village founded just after 1900 as use of the drover's road was beginning to decline. It sits on a dry ridge above the French Broad and Asheville.

ASHEVILLE is a place of note for many reasons, but it has its beginnings in the early 1820s as a sulphur spring resort. The first commissioners of the town may have set the original seat of government at a tavern where "Mountain Dew flowed freely."[69] The Biltmore House is probably the most outstanding attraction, an early castle built by George Vanderbilt between

Mountain Park Hotel in Hot Springs, North Carolina, at the beginning of the 1900s.

This church building in Walnut, North Carolina, has been the local Presbyterian church and the first county courthouse.

View of Marshall, a deep valley town along the French Broad River in western North Carolina, in the early 1900s.

1889 and 1895 and designed by Richard Morris Hunt with landscaping by Frederick Law Olmsted, both among the most recognized professionals of the time. The estate was serviced by Biltmore Village at the entrance. The historic stone Grove Park Inn opened in 1900 and continues to serve the public with fine accommodations. It was also used by the military during World War II. The River Arts District houses studios and galleries in the abandoned cotton manufacturing area along the river. Asheville was also the home of Thomas Wolfe and the location of his monumental work *Look Homeward, Angel*. Some history relevant to the Augusta Road and Dixie Highway is the path in downtown at Pack Square, where two drover's trails crossed. They have been marked by bronze sculptures of hogs and turkeys that once were driven down the trail to market. Also, a Dixie Highway marker helped designate the road's changes over time—from dirt stock turnpike to concrete interstate highway.

HENDERSONVILLE is the county seat of Henderson County, and the historic downtown was built at the turn of the twentieth century. The wide Main Street, laid out by slaves in the 1840s, provided plenty of room for the hordes of animals to pass through town.

FLAT ROCK, just south of Hendersonville, was one of the earliest vacation resorts for plantation owners from the Lowcountry of South Carolina. Many historic hotels of the stagecoach period and later motor courts along

Right: At Pack Square in Asheville, North Carolina, two drover's roads crossed. Now the trails are remembered with bronze sculptures of hogs and turkeys and their tracks along a preserved concrete path.

Below: The milk goat dairy at Connemara, the Sandburg Home in Flat Rock, North Carolina.

U.S. 25 can still be seen near downtown. One famous visitor who came and stayed was the poet Carl Sandburg. His home and the farm where his wife, Lilian, raised prized milk goats is a National Historic Site complete with descendants of that famous herd.

DOWN THE GAP

The Saluda Gap was one of the most challenging sites on the road for travelers. Bishop Asbury described Saluda Mountain: "The descent exceeds all I know from the province of Maine to Kentucky and Cumberland."[70]

TUXEDO is located near the state line and at the top of the Saluda Gap into South Carolina. Many travelers from the Lowcountry visited here in the nineteenth and early twentieth centuries. Sections of the stagecoach and drover's road can still be found here. After the War Between the States, a group of freedmen traveled from Mississippi to form a communal village they called the Kingdom of Happy Land and were a viable group important to the return of commerce along the road until nearly 1900 (see chapter 11).

North Saluda Reservoir in Upstate South Carolina covers the drover's trail town of Merrittsville.

The early Greenville County Library Bookmobile visited the Goodwin House Inn, circa 1930s. *Collection of the Greenville County Library.*

From Tuxedo, moving into South Carolina, the road winds down the gap. Part of this road was called "the winds." Below "the winds" came the tollbooth and then the camp at Merrittsville.

MERRITTSVILLE, named for Benjamin Merritt in a deed of 1799, was first a drover's stop and grew into a small village by the beginning of the 1900s when U.S. 25 was paved through the main street in 1928. This town was sacrificed to enlarge water collection for the city of Greenville in the early 1960s. Merrittsville is now covered by the North Saluda Reservoir and the entrance is blocked, but the roads into and out of Merrittsville can still be identified from Old U.S. 25 and Callahan Mountain Road.

GOODWIN HOUSE INN on Scenic Highway 11 just west of U.S. 25 was an early inn on the road to Augusta, and the exterior has been recently restored by Greenville County. The Preacher's Room on the front porch reminds visitors that Methodist Bishop Asbury stayed in this very inn even before it passed to the Goodwin family.

OVER THE RIDGE

The ridge was between the Reedy River and the Saluda River, both commencing in upper Greenville County.

TRAVELERS REST was just that in the mid-nineteenth century. An inn on the stagecoach road, later known as Spring Park, was enlarged in 1851 to accommodate travelers. After the railroad came to town, it was fashionable for Greenvillians to take picnics and catch the train there for a ride up

The Spring Park Inn in Travelers Rest, South Carolina, is in the National Register of Historic Places. *Collection of Kyle Campbell.*

the mountain and back, to enjoy music from the bandstand or to hear a politician speak. Much of downtown has been restored since the Swamp Rabbit Trail—the old railroad track turned into a walking/biking path—has revitalized the area.

GREENVILLE is now the largest city on U.S. Highway 25 in the Carolinas. The dirt trail to Augusta came through Main Street as with the other towns, but during the growth of the textile industry after the War Between the States, Greenville grew rapidly. The Main Street is much the same as it was in the first half of the twentieth century, with some new landscaping for parking. Reedy River Falls was the site of the first plantation cabin and has been a focal point of the growth of the city. Once called the "Mountain Town," Greenville began to flourish when wealthy Lowcountry planters came for the summers starting in the 1820s, and the Mansion House was the fine hotel near the falls. Later, when the road was paved and U.S. 25 came through, the Poinsett Hotel replaced the Mansion House, and the Ottaray and Dixie (later Imperial and Greenville) Hotels expanded the choices of accommodations for the upper class. Today, Greenville and Asheville are both destination cities.

From Greenville south on the stage road, the miles between villages increased through open rolling farmland and plantations along a ridge between the Reedy and Saluda Rivers.

Main Street, Greenville, South Carolina, circa 1900, with horse-drawn carriage, automobiles and horse-drawn trolley.

WOODVILLE and WARE PLACE were two small but important crossroads about fifteen miles south of Greenville. Woodville was home to the Woodside family of cotton mill fame. Ware Place was the plantation of T. Ed Ware, a state legislator in the mid-1800s, who acquired the house through his wife's family and was later convicted of killing his father-in-law during a domestic dispute with the daughter over the elder gentleman's remarriage. In what was called the trial of the century in Greenville County, Ware was convicted and then pardoned by the governor a week later. Another important note concerning Ware Place was the wired radio station that thrived from Chandler's store during the first part of the 1900s.[71]

MCCULLOUGH'S house and inn was a pleasant stop on the road about twenty-five miles south of Greenville. The Federal brick house was built in 1812 by Joseph McCullough and was where he raised his family and expanded the plantation to at least fifteen thousand acres. Standing about fifty feet from the current U.S. 25, the home was owned by the family until 2019 and is now being restored by the Fork Shoals Historical Society. Over the early 1800s, McCullough sponsored horse races that were run by the finest horses in the state, and the circus came to the plantation for entertaining the locals. Lowcountry visitors traveling to the mountains for summers stopped for some of the peach brandy crafted on site. And

The 1820 T. Edwin Ware House sits at a crossroads in southern Greenville County now called Ware Place. The image from a tintype shows Abner Sims and his father, William, near Ware Place, circa 1860–70. *Collection of Cheryl MacKnight.*

Around the turn of the twentieth century, Nan Scott Babb and Jo Ware are wrapped up for a chilly winter ride to Pelzer with a lap robe and gloves. *Collection of Nancy Rector.*

A view of the McCullough house, Cedarhurst, in the early 1900s during its Greek Revival period.

Stoney Point has been restored to its original beauty. Construction was begun in 1818, and it and the McCullough House (1812) were both of Federal design.

of course, the droves of cattle, hogs, mules and turkeys, as well as their drovers, stopped for the nights during the fall and winter.

CORONACA, now south of Lake Greenwood, has a name given by local Native Americans meaning "the place of the large white oaks." Some think the name is a corruption of "corn acre." It was at a crossroads in the early 1800s, and another inn along the road, Stoney Point, was a busy plantation similar to McCullough's. Stoney Point has been restored by a descendant of the original owners, the Joel Smiths.

NINETY SIX or CAMBRIDGE or the Star Fort is basically the same place. The Star Fort was built by Loyalists during the Revolution and is a National Historic Site. Cambridge was the site of an early school. The town of Ninety Six's name told the distance from the Lower Cherokee town of Keowee in the Cherokee Nation.

From here, the drover's road split into two possible choices to travel toward Edgefield.

ALONG THE FALL LINE

New challenges for travelers came along the South Carolina fall line.

MEETING STREET, the town on the road to the southeast, has an exciting story that is still told (see chapter 11).

KIRKSEY is to the southwest and on the current U.S. 25. Kirksey was a pottery-producing area at the time of the wagon road.

EDGEFIELD, known as the home of ten governors, probably has the longest recorded history of the towns on the Augusta Road, and many noted South Carolinians built luxury homes along the Buncombe Road just north of town during the 1800s. Many of these homes are still private residences. Trade was recorded here as early as the 1690s.[72] Best known for Jug Town and several other pottery sites, the area's clays drew several wealthy plantation owners into the business of utilitarian pottery for storage of food and drinks. Now famous, the literate slave potter Dave Drake worked at several sites just outside town.

Edgefield lies on the fall line, with clay soils to the northwest growing forests of oak and hickory and the lands to the southeast allowing long-needle pines to grow in ancient ocean sands. These different types of soil forced different paths to Augusta to be used in different weather conditions. The sands were difficult for narrow wagon wheels to maneuver, but the

The Brooks-Tompkins Home on Buncombe Street in Edgefield, South Carolina, is among a number of early 1800s mansions along the road.

clays to the northwest, when wet, became impassable. Therefore, from the Edgefield area there were three roads leading to Augusta/Hamburg.

TRENTON is on U.S. 25 in the sandy southeast, a flat land now covered in peach orchards. At the stop where the road turns toward the Savannah River is the Pine House, which originated in 1757 and was enlarged over the nineteenth century into a lovely, stately mansion. It was initially a cabin and tavern in the backwoods during the colonial period and is now in the care of descendants of early owners. A stone road marker from the 1840s can be seen in the yard near U.S. 25 marking twenty miles to Augusta.[73]

OLD STAGE ROAD exits Edgefield to the west and was one of the first two roads across Edgefield County. Its meetinghouse, Horn's Creek Church, was founded in 1768 and can be seen along this public dirt road.[74]

SWEETWATER ROAD runs between Old Stage and Martintown Roads and is a pleasant drive.

MARTINTOWN ROAD bypasses Edgefield on the north and west. It leads to Augusta/Hamburg from Kirksey. It was one of the two earliest passageways for hunters and drovers. By 1715, a cattle drover, John Stevens, had established a cow pen at the head of what is still known as Steven's Creek.[75] Hardy's Church was established on this trail in 1762.[76]

This is a stone road marker from the mid-1800s at the Pine House in Trenton, South Carolina. It tells travelers that Augusta and Hamburg are twenty miles away.

Old Stage Road in Edgefield County led to Augusta, Georgia, and the port on the Savannah River.

Hampton Terrace Hotel sat on a cliff overlooking the Savannah River. This began the town of North Augusta, South Carolina, near the old port of Hamburg. By 1900, Hamburg was overtaken by the new village of North Augusta.

HAMBURG on the Savannah River was built in 1821 by Henry Shultz, who named it for his hometown in Germany. Designed as a rival port for Augusta, it thrived on the South Carolina side of the Savannah River at the original site of old Savannah Town. Then the town of Augusta built a canal, bringing much trade back across the river to Georgia. In the 1830s, the Phoenix, the first long-distance train from Charleston, was constructed to siphon off the cotton trade going to Savannah, Georgia. Again, in the 1850s, the South Carolina Canal and Railroad Company continued its line to Augusta, and Hamburg's cotton was diverted. Following the war in 1876, Hamburg was the site of a massacre of freed Blacks over voting suppression. Later, a luxury hotel was built on a bluff above the river, and at the turn of the 1900s, it became a vacation spot for northerners traveling the railroad line. This evolved into the new town of North Augusta, which was incorporated in 1906 and soon engulfed the old port of Hamburg, turning it into a ghost town.[77]

Hamburg was the end of the trail in South Carolina.

Chapter 3

GROWTH ALONG THE ROAD

The Coming of Mules, Conestogas and Stages

N ear the mid-nineteenth century, South Carolina's Upstate was becoming a major center of wealth for some, while up the Buncombe Turnpike in North Carolina, the road was beginning to bring visitors and trade as well. Farming was still the major industry, built on subsistence farms and plantation slave labor, with some manufacturing, gristmills and cotton gins. But the tie for much of this trade was the road to Hamburg and Augusta. Along the wagon road in oxcarts, Conestoga wagons, horse and mule trains and animal droves, settlers were buying and selling and traveling back and forth from home to camps, stands, mills, stores, trading posts, taverns, inns, hotels and resorts. The road was a busy place. Some of these travelers often passed the main town on the route, Greenville, on the west on a path named after a sign hanging on one of the taverns. White Horse Road is now Bypass U.S. 25. The tavern was near the Old Ebenezer School on Old White Horse Road just south of the new middle and high schools. White Horse Road Extension comes back into U.S. 25 north of Travelers Rest.

COMMERCE: FARM TO MARKET IN THE FALL AND WINTER

At the end of the growing season, backcountry farmers had their products ready to go to market—the closest market they could find—most often

Hamburg or Augusta. At the coming of cooler weather when the crops were being harvested and the stock had grown fat after grazing on the "balds,"[78] where hundreds of acres across the Appalachians were covered in sumptuous grasses, the cattle and hog men would figure their best advantage and decide whether to sell to a drover or drive the animals themselves. Although some farm products were carried to the ports, their grains were most often used in the home and by the families, and gristmills dotted the landscape along the shoals of large streams. Some tobacco and food stuffs like peaches, watermelons, nuts and corn were grown as well. Alcohol products were produced for local consumption—whiskey from corn and brandy from fruit.

Skins and furs remained important trade products in the South during the beginning decades of the nation, but as settlers moved into the backcountry and cleared land for farming, homegrown goods were traded. Farm wagons were not often owned yet, but sleds and carts pulled by oxen were the most prolific along the road. Early on, as trade began to move down the road, farmers brought their own food and feed for their stock and camped out where the land was flat and water and wood available. If the market was a good distance away, families and neighbors traveled together for protection, aid, and comradery. When they could afford a wagon, they attached removable ribs and covers for some shield from the elements.[79]

Bales of cotton brought to Charleston were shipped to New England or Great Britain before the cotton mill industry grew in the late 1800s.

This 1903 scene in a southern town was typical at the turn of the 1900s. City streets began being paved about 1905 in larger towns but not usually with concrete. Cotton seed was a plentiful commodity.

These farmers' cotton would be sold to the Greenwood Textile Mill or put on the train to Charleston. The Greenville and Columbia Railroad was built through Greenwood in the early 1850s prior to the construction of the mill.

Even from the far reaches of Kentucky, stock and wagons of produce moved down the drover's trail through the Carolinas to Hamburg toward the cities along the coast. Charleston was a farther trek, resulting in stock losing weight and eating more. The cost of droving to that town was often more than owners were willing to forego. Another consideration was the time it took for the round trip. Some of the mountain folk spent three to four months carrying products to market, trading for essentials like thread, coffee and spices for life at home and returning with wagons loaded on the trip back uphill. Along the way, the travelers found companionship and adventure, but not always to their liking. Even innkeepers were hanged for robbing and murdering their patrons.[80]

Droves and droves and droves of cattle, hogs, turkeys, ducks, horses and mules came down from Tennessee and Kentucky along the road to Hamburg or Augusta in the frosty weather each year. The camp or "stand" owners began to provide pens for the animals and occasional lean-to shelters for the drovers, and locals brought feed for the stock. Stands could be large compounds of numerous pens, enclosures and outbuildings. These droves, particularly pigs, included tens of thousands a year. Swine would block the road for hours at a time as five hundred to ten thousand could pass in one drove, and there might be five or six droves in a day, grunting and squealing all the way. Hogs are always hungry, and if they were not pushed onward, they would stop and root. Then again, if they stampeded, the drovers had to let them run until they dropped or stopped on their own. Turkeys in large flocks of three to six hundred were more of a challenge to drivers. Someone had to ride in front dropping shelled corn occasionally as incentive for the fowl to move forward. Drivers kept to the sides and back using long whips. At the end of the day, the flock would be fed and then scatter into trees to roost for the night.[81]

Although the herds were not as numerous, the horse and mule trade was as lucrative. Horse and mule droves of one hundred from Kentucky and even Ohio were regarded as fine specimen. Horse racing was a popular sport along the road, with tracks at McCullough's and Aiken, and horse theft or murder was a hanging offense. The mules were described as fine as of those in Spain and Portugal. Mules took over the duties of the oxen on the farms of the South after George Washington and Henry Clay began purchasing breeding donkeys and horses in Europe in the early 1800s and promoting them for farmwork.[82] Because breeding to raise mules was not an easy chore, most Carolina farmers chose not to breed but to purchase, which increased the numbers coming down from breeders in Kentucky and Tennessee.[83] To

Mule day market in Mayfield, Kentucky, circa 1915.

a subsistence farmer or plantation owner, the mule was a prized possession, necessary for life. An average one cost $230, while a fine specimen could go for up to $1,000 in the mid-1800s, an exorbitant sum at that time.[84]

Taverns and inns opened along the drover's road as in Hot Springs; some were gracious and safe, while others were not. Choosing wisely was imperative. Large stands usually included a tavern, inn or inn/farmhouse where the drover would stay. The drivers working for him were usually youths who had a bunkhouse or small cabin or possibly a lean-to where they slept on pallets. As the drovers moved down the mountains with the stock drives, they were swapping and dealing as they went. When an animal faltered, it was bartered to the innkeepers for the drover's overnight accommodations and animal feed, thus feeding the next travelers on the road.

Money was rarely needed along the trail. Waggoneers sold products by traveling from town to crossroads hawking such goods as ceramic jugs, whiskey and "likker," tobacco, cane sugar and "bunch yarn" used for knitting. The innkeepers, drovers and drummers—dealing in pots and pans, needles and thread, mirrors and pocketknives, thimbles and scissors, cloth and patterns and medicines—traded not only goods but also stories, news, music and songs.[85] Downtimes were spent in entertainment in the inns and in the roadside campsites as well. Some early maps even designated taverns as entertainment.

If cotton was grown on a subsistence farm, it was usually for the pioneer women to make the family's clothing and bedding. But for the plantations on the lower end of the road to Augusta in the early 1800s, cotton became a crop of importance in the rich, newly cleared soil and was lucrative trade primarily shipped to northern cotton mills.

In the larger town of Greenville, many of these farmers and drovers had to overnight at the edge of town. Soon, merchants decided to accommodate these traders with a wagon shed one hundred feet long and forty-five feet wide with eighty stalls and feed troughs. The roof was built to allow for wagons piled with cotton, and one such warehouse had sleeping quarters in the roof. Soon, too, taverns, hotels and boardinghouses opened to the farmers and drovers as the village grew.[86]

Travel: Vacationers in the Spring and Summer

By 1820, wealthy Lowcountry plantation owners had become a staple of upcountry and mountain summers. Stagecoach routes were prevalent. The "Mountain Town" of Greenville and the North Carolina border town of Flat Rock were enjoying an influx of culture and money, although some debated the culture piece. The elite had to travel the road usually from at least Ninety Six, if not Edgefield or Augusta, to come to the Upstate. Some did come up the new State Road as well, although portions of it between Columbia and Greenville County were not well kept, and travelers mostly used the free roads paralleling it.[87]

Outbreaks of malaria prior to 1800 in the Lowcountry sent many aristocrats into the Upstate and mountains from late spring to the first frost of autumn. They came by all routes and in many forms of transport. They stayed with family and friends; in boardinghouses, hotels and resorts; and many built or purchased fine summer homes. Two of the first were Governors Henry Middleton and Joseph Alston. A number of these homes were constructed west of town between Buncombe Road and White Horse Road. The year 1815 brought the first real effort to profit from these visitors when Edmund Waddell rented prominent Greenvillian Vardry McBee's Prospect Hill estate to open a hotel. Then in 1824, William Toney, the wealthiest citizen of the area, constructed the brick Mansion House Hotel for their convenience. It quickly became the center of activity, but one resident felt that "the visitors are disposed to gratify their animal propensies without cultivating their interests at all, if they have any to cultivate."[88] Nonetheless, these visitors brought money and activity and knowledge of the backcountry of both Carolinas to the forefront in Lowcountry concerns. Caravans of these elites traveling with family and friends arrived with mounted escorts, numerous servants and slaves. They came in their own carriages and four-horse coaches with baggage wagons and outriders of eight or ten horses for a family.

At that time, there were three lines of stagecoaches coming to Greenville three times a week from Augusta, Columbia and Asheville, including Rumbough's from Warm Springs. Coachmen would blow the arrival on a horn announcing the number of visitors to prepare for, and then they would bring the stage to a stop in a wide sweep in front of the Mansion House. The Saluda and Buncombe Turnpikes drew travelers into North Carolina, to Flat Rock; Deaver's Springs, which was five miles west of Asheville; and Warm Springs.[89] Lured to the springs' curative powers and the mountain air, these fashionable visitors returned regularly.[90]

Asheville, prior to the War Between the States, was a small village along the turnpike, like Marshall, where there were two insignificant hotels, and the population included about three hundred whites and two hundred slaves. But just west, Sulphur Springs, or Deaver's Springs as it was later called, grew yearly from its beginning in 1827 after the turnpike was completed. At its best, five hundred visitors summered at the springs. Most were from South Carolina, including the Pinckneys from the Lowcountry and the Pickenses from the Upstate. Yearly from May to frost, the Charleston Alstons reserved corner rooms with the best view.[91]

S.S. Crittenden suggests in *The Greenville Century Book, 1903*, "That it was through the influence in the legislature of the low country visitors to Greenville and Flat Rock that the State Road to Columbia and Charleston was built through this county across the mountains at Saluda Gap,"[92] bringing prosperity to many Upstate and North Carolina locals.

FARMS AND PLANTATIONS

Along the lower trail to Augusta prior to the war years, cotton plantations prospered, and cotton farming gradually moved up the road into the Upstate by 1825 or so. These early settlers were mainly poor farmers without the assistance of slaves who raised large families to work the land. The larger property owners after the first quarter of the century began to acquire slaves and plant cotton as well as food crops, and they began to see enough surplus staple cotton to transport it to Hamburg's port. As this production moved north in South Carolina along the road, plantations around Edgefield, Ninety Six, Coronaca and into Greenville County began to prosper.

This commerce with the owners traveling back and forth to Hamburg on about a twenty-mile horseback ride each day provided opportunities for these gentlemen to visit friends along the road. For instance, the Joseph McCullough family on the road south of Greenville visited the Smiths at Stoney Point Plantation in Coronaca, also on the road about twenty miles south, often enough to have two children marry, thus tying the families together. Also, the two plantation houses are of almost the exact same brick Federal design, with McCullough's a few years older (1812 to 1818).

These plantations were almost completely self-sufficient communities with the aid of the slaves. Evidence shows that at the McCullough House, slaves had an important presence in the lives of the family. Three cemeteries exist on the property; one for the family is fenced; one next to that and also fenced is for the house slaves; and the third, not far away, is for the field slaves. Other local farms often include slaves buried in the family cemetery. Slave quarters were often located in close proximity to the plantation house, as can be seen on early plats. After the Haitian slave rebellion in 1791, many slaves were bred in Virginia for sale in the Deep South.[93] Enslaved Africans were brought along the road to Augusta by traders, and auctions were held along the road. One such group left a disgruntled young woman with twins at a plantation near the Augusta Road. Her husband had been left behind. Two years later, as she worked the field along the road, another group passed. Seeing her husband among the group, she was overjoyed when her master purchased the husband and father to reunite the family.[94] That didn't usually happen, for many families were separated, and after the war, those who were able searched for years for beloved family members.

In the backcountry of South Carolina, these well-to-do families often used silver and English china, and furniture was crafted on site or purchased in Charleston. Gristmills and later cotton gins were close by, and some brick kilns and blacksmith shops were available. Also, plantation inns usually supported small stores, as did both the McCullough and Goodwin inns at opposite ends of Greenville County.

Schools were not readily available for these families, but tutors were part of the culture. Slave houses often were clapboard buildings with a center dividing wall containing a central chimney with a fireplace on each side and exit door for each room. In one instance, a slave house near the road

Holly Spring Colored School, situated in southern Greenville County, was purchased in 1891 by the school trustees and was closed in 1951 during the equalization of schools in South Carolina. Segregated schools continued until 1970. It was recently restored and is now in the National Register.

later became the first public school for African Americans in the southern part of Greenville County. Holly Spring School (built prior to 1891) has recently been restored and placed in the National Register of Historic Places by Holly Spring Baptist Church with help from the Fork Shoals Historical Society.[95]

Poor farmers along the Hamburg/Augusta Road grew the same kinds of crops found on large plantations, but without slave help. These resourceful families needed little money, for they grew their meat, including cattle, hogs and poultry, or traded feed crops for them along the road. Food crops included corn, tomatoes, greens of all kinds, wheat and some fruit, such as North Carolina apples and South Carolina peaches. These subsistence farmers also produced alcoholic drinks for extra trade products when needed. Sheep were kept for wool, and flax was grown for linen, as well as small amounts of cotton to turn into clothing. One common rough material, linsey-woolsey, was made from both linen and wool, and the wool was often dyed with indigo. This made a lightweight but warm material often used for bedcovers as well as winter clothing.

THE ANTEBELLUM ROAD

Along the lower portions of the Augusta Road in the flatter lands and rolling hills of South Carolina during the antebellum period, production of cotton came to the forefront of plantation and farming life. During this time, the numbers of enslaved African peoples grew and Native American slaves decreased in the western parts of the Carolinas. This was also a time of going west—farther west—to the newly opened lands of the Louisiana Purchase. Many Carolinians packed up everything, sold lands and traveled west in covered wagons. Those who stayed behind planted cotton. New settlers continued to come into the backcountry, helping to stabilize the population. Most were subsistence farmers; some were plantation owners with thousands of acres of tillable land.

The enslaved population lived under travel restrictions unlike the freedom of movement whites enjoyed. For the white population, freedom of movement was part of their Constitutional rights and was verified by the Supreme Court, but Blacks lived under the Black codes drafted in the individual states that regulated slave movement and restricted them to their masters' property most of their lives.[96] Some slaves with specific skills were allowed to travel with their products to a market, as was the case of Edgefield potter Dave Drake, who would travel to Hamburg and the train to deliver loads of pots to plantations across South Carolina and Georgia.[97] Some were given metal tags on a chain for identification and as a pass, but most carried a paper signed by their owner.

These permissions were the only way enslaved persons could travel, and slave patrols formed to enforce the Black codes, with these squads checking for signed papers for passage. They stopped all Black persons, enslaved or free, in order to keep the slaves in line for their owners. Some of these enslaved persons would creep through the woods at night in order to visit family, taking unbelievable chances. If captured without a pass, a slave could be lashed even before returning him to his owner, thus sending fear and intimidation throughout the population. Cotton was becoming the

This advertisement for a plank road shows two of the many uses of the drover's road: a tobacco hogshead and a stagecoach. Greenville News, *June 13, 1954, 32.*

main crop in the South, and moving it to market did allow some slaves to see parts of the world off the plantation.[98]

The cotton was being transported down the road and then to Britain or New England cotton mills, but some entrepreneurs began to consider the possibility of producing cotton goods in the South. It was the height of raw cotton production and the beginning of the sheeting industry in the South. The Augusta/Buncombe Road became a path to the cotton mills of western South Carolina, and mills began to open near it in the Upstate and later in North Carolina. One of the first cotton mills in the upstate (1824) was on the Reedy River at Fork Shoals, approximately four miles from the Augusta/Hamburg Road. In the town of Graniteville, near the road between Edgefield and Augusta, the first large mill proved that manufacturing could be lucrative in the South.

INDUSTRY

Industry was the new interest of the moneyed entrepreneurs in the antebellum South. Cotton mills in Britain and New England were flourishing, and northerners and southerners wanted to get in on that growth. Northern mills needed the cotton that was grown in the South with cheap slave labor, and southerners became tied to this trade for the money. Soon southern plantation owners wanted to try their hands at the manufacture of cotton goods themselves. Small cotton mills were attempted by the 1820s in the Upstate, but the most successful was the Graniteville mill near Trenton, South Carolina, not far from part of the lower end of the drover's road to Hamburg/Augusta.

The cotton industry in South Carolina began by producing and exporting cotton to New England mills. One issue that became evident to businessmen in Charleston was that most of the cotton was grown in the backcountry, but Charleston, being an important port, was not the backcountry outlet that Savannah, Georgia, was since it was on the great Savannah River dividing the two states. It was much easier and closer for farmers to transport their cotton to Hamburg on the South Carolina side of the Savannah and send it downriver on a flatboat than to bring it to Charleston by wagon train.[99] Therefore, Savannah was flourishing, and the road to Hamburg was full of cotton wagons at times backed up a quarter of a mile or more to unload.

Early industry in Greenville County is shown by the Fork Shoals Cotton Mill, which was established circa 1820 by Shubal Arnold and ran under several owners over 150 years of creating textiles in southern Greenville County. *Greenville County Recreation Department and Fork Shoals Historical Society.*

In 1827, the South Carolina Canal and Railroad Company was formed in order to divert cotton commerce from the upcountry to the Charleston port. The train, the Phoenix, finally reached Hamburg in October 1833 and traveled the longest track in the world at 136 miles. The success of this endeavor was gratifying to Charleston's port until a canal was built in Augusta, and later, other longer rail systems were constructed in the 1850s.[100]

Several small cotton mills were established in Greenville County in 1820. One, the Arnold-Berry mill, was near the drover's road in southern Greenville on the Reedy River, and another was near the State Road being built in the northern part of the county, Weaver Factory. The Weaver Factory and some others that followed, such as the William Bates Company, were developed by northerners coming into the Greenville District to start mills on the swift waterways.[101] In the southern part of the county, the Arnolds and Berrys had moved into the Fork Shoals area from Laurens and had been merchants and plantation owners in the area for decades.[102] These factories were minimally successful, coming in and then going out of business or being sold numerous times.

A reproduction of the first regularly scheduled railroad train in South Carolina and America, the Best Friend of Charleston, was built in 1928 and appeared in the Tricentennial Parade in 1970.

Then the first enormously successful enterprise opened in a small town in Aiken County just south of the road to Hamburg, about twenty miles away. The Graniteville mill was the work of William Gregg and was constructed in 1845. Gregg's success encouraged other backcountry entrepreneurs to invest in cotton manufacturing, and the waterways began to be investigated for possible sites. Engineers studied the state's rivers and streams in 1880, making recommendations for industry[103] with the hope of instituting manufacturing to reignite prosperity in South Carolina after the war.

NEW ROAD BUILDING AND MAINTENANCE

The road to Augusta or Hamburg began to be worn out and in places significantly damaged from the growth in traffic. Foot traffic and pack trains changed to ever-increasing numbers of hooves, horse trains, wagon trains and stagecoaches, not counting local wagons and carriages, horses, mules and oxen. Improving the road was one issue, but maintaining that better road was another.

Corduroy Roads

Over the years, the condition of the road had depended on the weather and the geography. As the early paths and trails had avoided creeks, bogs, rocks and sand, if possible, the added movement over weak spots caused areas to disintegrate. If the low area was damp, in the rain it became a swamp. If the ground was sand, as in the Edgefield location to the east toward the Pine House, it could become quicksand. One remedy that was often used in these expanses was to cover it with logs. Trees were plentiful and cheap, and the trunks usually provided a way to keep from getting bogged down in sand or mud. But this building material did not provide a good wagon or stage ride even when covered with sand or mud to level. Thus, they became known as "corduroy" roads. Usually the riders had to dismount their steeds and, sometimes, the vehicle to cross.

One visitor described South Carolina roads as the worst in the early states. He stated that the rotting corduroy roads could cause his horse to suddenly sink to its belly in the mud below, or sometimes the wet, slick muck put the logs to spinning when stepped on and would cause the animal to break a leg.[104] Initially, the State Road from Charleston to Columbia was a corduroy road. One description of riding this new thoroughfare by Reverend Abbott in 1828 was that

> *the small logs were split in half flat side up and covered with a few inches of clayey sand....this kind of road keeps your bodies in a perpetual quiver, and you are left to apprehend that your brains may be shaken out of place or addled....The toll is duly collected...so that you have the pleasure of being well shaken and of paying for it.*[105]

This description could well be applied to the Edgefield area of the road to Augusta.

Plank Roads

In the northern states during the 1830s and 1840s, another concept to improve the roads was the "plank road." This process was adopted in the South and often involved just adding planks over the logs, but sometimes the road was reconstructed to an engineered design. The idea was to allow travel to be smooth and progress more rapid for the wagons moving along the road. Several towns along the drover's road became interested in constructing plank roads, particularly Hamburg to Edgefield and Greenville to Asheville.[106]

> *Workers first graded a roadbed. Then they elevated the center of the road so that water could drain. Measuring approximately five by eight feet, wooden sills were laid next as support. After that, pine planks measuring approximately eight feet long and eight inches wide and four inches thick were laid on top of the sills. Laws required the roads to be a minimum of eight feet and a maximum of sixty feet, and typically plank roads were eight feet wide and adjacent to a well-graded dirt road. Avoiding getting stuck in the mud, teamsters traveled on the planks, while individuals and light carriages passed on the dirt road.[107]*

Also, the planks might be covered with small gravel or coarse sand, and with the horse droppings, the surface compacted into a hard, tough covering.[108]

Plank roads were usually privately funded toll roads. Having another lane alongside the plank road often enticed the wagons, especially on return trips, to take the side road to cut costs taking money from the road builder. When the plank roads from Hamburg to Edgefield (twenty-six miles was the longest in South Carolina) and Cheatham were completed in 1856, news articles implored citizens to use the new toll roads to support the builders who were required to maintain them as well.[109] Bridge tolls were necessary too, so all along the way, travelers were required to pay or barter for further progress.

> *The old [Smith] bridge [below Asheville] was a single-track affair without handrails for a long time before the Civil War, and nothing but log stringers on each side of the roadway. Col. J.C. Smathers of the Turnpike remembers when, if a team began to back, there was nothing to prevent a vehicle going over into the river.[110]*

This bridge was on the Asheville to Greenville Plank Road built in 1851, but only the portion from the Saluda Gap to Asheville was completed in North Carolina.[111] Passing on the Asheville part, a traveler from Edgefield stated that his hometown plank roads were much superior, with the width at least a foot wider, the grade much easier and the ride much smoother.[112]

Maintaining the roads had been hard since the beginning of the country. Continuing to hold feelings of mistrust of those in control, the citizens of the young Carolinas hindered federal government supervision of the growing

Plank roads were built in the Carolinas in the 1840s and 1850s to aid in heavy wagon transportation. As seen in this photograph, most had a dirt trail alongside as an alternative. Many wagons that were returning with a lighter load chose to use the side road to avoid tolls. *North Carolina Business History—Plank Road.*

numbers of passageways. Therefore, local agencies were left in control and generally bungled the upkeep for one hundred years.[113] Commonly, local males were conscripted to spend a specific number of days each year working on roads along their own sections of a path. Most wealthy men sent slaves or paid others to cover their commitment, but when they did not, it was often overlooked, so essentially Black men maintained the roads. Later, state legislatures gave permission for persons or groups to oversee road building and upkeep, and to cover this work, they were allowed to collect tolls from travelers on their allotted section. Backcountry areas often fought with the Lowcountry over road issues, for they were totally dependent on ground transportation. When public agencies began to take over some bridges and plank roads, those and the turnpikes as well were all left to decay. Without governance and oversight and policing, these efforts were weak, to say the least, and full of graft, and the roads broke down.

Conestoga Wagons

Particularly relevant to the maintenance of the road to Hamburg and Augusta was the Conestoga wagon. These great vehicles of burden, first crafted about 1750, became the main moving van of the westward expansion and of commerce in the 1800s. Able to transport three tons of goods and people on four-inch-wide wheels and pulled by four to six draft animals, these massive wagons carried cotton and other products to Augusta and Hamburg, mainly in the fall. The ruts from this traffic can still be found along the route. Following the end of the cotton season, the passageways

The Conestoga wagon was designed for heavy loads up to six tons. This smaller version shows the covering for weather protection.

could be regraded to provide a smoother ride for a time. For the areas with corduroy or plank roads, one hundred Conestogas could pass in a day, taking precedent over other vehicles and leaving the road itself worn.

Another interesting aspect of the Conestoga wagon is that it may be the reason Americans drive on the right side of the road while those in Great Britain drive on the left. When possible, these four-wheeled wagons with large covers tended to be driven in the center of the roadway, and the design of the craft put the driver on the left, riding the horse nearest the wheel and ready to operate the brake, which was always on the left. Therefore, the Conestoga tended to be driven on the right of center, and since other carriages and lighter vehicles followed in the ruts behind the wagons, other drivers became accustomed to the right side of the road too. When the State Road was proposed from Charleston to Columbia in 1824, a statute ruled that all traffic should keep to the right of center of the road. This had been the practice in northern states as early as 1810.[114]

Chapter 4

ADVERSITY

Preparing the Way

D uring the War Between the States, the plank roads were basically demolished and the roads returned to dirt.[115] Reconstruction at first provided African Americans some power in the state legislatures, but that soon was reneged upon. All groups—poor whites, freed peoples, plantation owners—went through an adjustment period. Economically, the whole South was devastated. In order to aid in the restoration of some semblance of a sustainable livelihood, investors in cotton mills began to lead in bringing the industry up the Augusta Road along the waterways. Drovers continued their trips leading stock to Hamburg and Augusta, and the town of North Augusta, South Carolina, emerged to overtake Hamburg's port. Farming evolved into a sharecropping existence for most Blacks and poor whites.

As manufacturing grew in the Upstate of South Carolina, many mountain folk moved into positions as operatives in mills around Greenville. New Englanders familiar with cotton manufacturing took leadership positions in southern mills, and mill engineers and architects were brought south as well. With this manufacturing growth, farming in Upstate South Carolina centered on the cotton crop coming into the mills from the countryside mainly on farm-to-market roads, with some traveling to ocean ports on trains.

A mule team pulls a wagonload of cow and horse hides to Piedmont Manufacturing Company, circa 1920. *Piedmont Historical Collection in the Don Roper Museum.*

MANUFACTURING

The cotton manufacturing industry in the Upstate of South Carolina was supported by northern industrial machinery manufacturers, engineers and architects, along with local cotton production. Since the first mill at Graniteville near Aiken not far off the road to Augusta/Hamburg had shown that cotton sheeting products could be a moneymaking business, one Upstate entrepreneur and son-in-law of a small mill owner from New England, H.P. Hammett, envisioned a large mill on the Saluda River at Garrison Shoals. The owner of the Graniteville mill, William Gregg, lent his support for Hammett's work through his brother, a Lowcountry plantation owner, who was on the board at the beginning of the Saluda site. Hammett's efforts to establish the first mill at the new village of Piedmont came to fruition in 1876 when the first sheeting from the Piedmont Manufacturing Company was run. The success of this mill led to Hammett continuing to build three more full-size mills at the site by 1895. Called the kindergarten of Greenville manufacturing because many presidents of mills across the Upstate and western North Carolina were trained there, Piedmont was the model endeavor. If it had not been for the success at Piedmont, Greenville would not have become the Textile Center of the World during the first half of the twentieth century. This shoals site was south of Greenville, four miles from the road to Augusta, surrounded by cow pens and beside the track of the Greenville and Columbia Railroad. Transportation for the Piedmont cotton goods was ensured.[116]

From this start, mills sprang up across the Upstate, with downtown Greenville's west side along the Buncombe Highway (early U.S. 25) becoming the locus.[117] The Greenville and Columbia Railroad came to the Upstate in 1853, and then in 1887, when Greenville's cotton mill industry began to flourish, the Greenville, Knoxville and Western Railroad Company was formed to bring coal from Tennessee to Augusta through the Upstate to support the cotton mills' energy production. The company president was J.B. Humbert of Princeton, South Carolina, with other officers from Greenville and Augusta. About fourteen miles of track was laid from Greenville through Travelers Rest by the Spring Park Inn to the village of Marietta. Many miles of grading had been completed as well before the construction company failed. These railroad cuts are still visible near Princeton and the McCullough House Inn along the Augusta Road and in northern parts of the county toward Brevard, North Carolina. This track would have followed

This Piedmont Manufacturing Company letterhead, circa 1900, shows the four full mills on both sides of the Saluda in Greenville and Anderson Counties of Upstate South Carolina. A National Historical Landmark, it burned in 1982, but the turn-of-the-century downtown still stands and is being restored.

the dirt Augusta Road from Augusta to Travelers Rest and then veered to the west to cross the mountains to Knoxville through Jones Gap.[118]

With the road and the trains leading to Greenville, these mills flourished, and many investors and operatives did so as well. African Americans worked for the cotton industry but were basically on the loading docks doing the hardest manual labor. In the Upstate, these now defunct mill buildings are being restored for downtown housing, and along the French Broad in Asheville, the mills are the center of the restorative River Arts District. Greenwood Manufacturing in the new town of Greenwood came into being during the late 1800s after the coming of the railroads.[119] Just after the turn of the century, Riegel Manufacturing built the town of Ware Shoals on another Saluda River site. The power along the Augusta Road grew from the cotton fields and sheeting goods selling across the world, even to China.[120]

RELIGION AND EDUCATION

Several churches were established along the road to Augusta that are still important in their respective communities. Horn's Creek Baptist Church on the Old Stage Road near Edgefield was established in 1768, and a building was raised by 1784. Another was Lickville Presbyterian in lower Greenville County along the Augusta Road. It was built in 1882 and still overlooks the road today. The name comes from a salt lick just north of the church. An interesting church on the drover's road in North Carolina is the historic Walnut Presbyterian Church at the old site of Jewel Hill near Hot Springs.

Prior to the War Between the States, most education of children was done in the home by parents or tutors. There were a few churches that opened during the week for small groups of students and a single teacher. Some churches opened their doors to enslaved members, despite southern laws that forbid their education, although some enslaved groups and slave owners did educate quietly. At the end of the war, freedmen and women established their own churches in brush arbors and in homes. By the late 1800s, many of those congregations had built their own houses of worship. And feeling that education was the path to real freedom, they began their own one-room schoolhouses. Sometimes they purchased the property and started a school in an existing structure.

Holly Spring School is just such a school near the Augusta Road. Probably constructed during the 1850s as a slave cabin, by 1891, it was a thriving school and was opened a year prior to the local white school. In the 1920s and 1930s, African Americans took advantage of support from Sears-Roebuck Company and constructed Rosenwald Schools along the road. Evidence of one of these, Chapman Grove School, can be found just off the Augusta Road near Fork Shoals. Many one-teacher schools served both African American students and white ones, but not together. Segregation continued through the equalization of schools in the 1950s. Equalization closed the one-room schools, built new buildings and bused students some distances to still-separate schools. Not until 1970 did school segregation begin to disappear along the road.

Following Gregg's model for his cotton mill and village at Graniteville, Upstate mill owners created a society of paternalism that mandated sobriety, church attendance and some school attendance for working children even prior to 1900. Although white children often worked, the mill opened small schools in the churches they had built for the operatives. The African American mill employees' children were not included. African American churches developed along the margins of the white mill villages and thrived, aiding in the education of their congregations.

In the postbellum South, some changes were taking place, especially in the growth of industry and commerce. As far as farming went, the focus on cotton production guided the way.

PART II

PAVING THE WAY

Driving the paving of the road was the automobile. This one was found at a mid-century gas station on the Old U.S. 25 on Main Street in Marshall, North Carolina.

Chapter 5

GOOD ROADS

The Push, the People and the Politics

The condition of South Carolina's roads was a topic across the country when a midwestern newspaper, the *Decatur County [KS] News*, shared the plight of farmers on January 27, 1896: "A Practical Road Lesson—Towns in South Carolina, located near the state line and not far from Charlotte, NC, have lost much trade of late, as the farmers prefer to haul over the good roads into another state in preference to using the poor roads of their own state. This experience has been instrumental in inaugurating a movement for good roads in South Carolina."

Travel was grueling and drawn-out. Some early improvements were the corduroy and plank roads, but maintenance was still a major problem. State fines were levied for not keeping up your section of the way. By the 1890s, a Progressive-era movement was sweeping across the states. Called the Good Roads Movement, this grassroots effort was in full force by 1900, especially with the invention of the automobile. Concrete was the choice pavement of this forceful group.[121] It is the hardest of the materials used to surface roads, and it is the hardest to eliminate when a road is moved or a bridge is rebuilt. Thus, concrete evidence is still extant across the interstate U.S. Highway 25 motorway.

Good Roads of Greenville County,
Greenville, S. C.

Newly paved concrete roads were used in advertising Greenville textiles around 1910. Good Roads to Greenville!

THE PUSH

The Good Roads Movement was actually begun by bicyclists and motorcyclists in the late 1800s,[122] and good roads were in demand across the nation as numbers of rubber-wheeled vehicles increased. The movement was taken over by the automobile industry as production increased rapidly after the turn of the twentieth century. By that time, autos were beginning to be seen as an important means of transportation and mud roads as the main hindrance to pleasant travel.[123]

The Dixie Highway and U.S. 25, the United States Highway System, were the culmination of the Progressive Good Roads Movement, active from the 1890s to the late 1920s, when the federal government set up the numbered interstate system. Historian Tammy Ingram purports that farmers and businessmen, northerners and southerners were united for many years in their support of the Good Roads Movement, and although the railroads built in the South in the 1850s supported the growth of the southern textile industry after the War Between the States, this mill industry depended primarily on local roads.

These mud ways brought the cotton to the rails, and the earliest textile mills in South Carolina at Graniteville and around Greenville were near the

Left: Initially, the bicycle and motorcycle men of the 1890s pushed the Good Roads Movement. Then, as more automobiles were acquired throughout the country, rubber-tired vehicles became the transportation mode of choice. *Greenville County Library Collection.*

Below: Cotton wagons line up at the office of Piedmont Manufacturing Company. *Piedmont Historical Collection in the Don Roper Museum.*

Buncombe/Augusta Road, which became U.S. Highway 25. President James L. Orr of the Piedmont Manufacturing Company south of Greenville stated at the turn of the 1900s that he bought all the cotton within a fifteen-mile radius of his mill, which was about four miles from the Augusta Road.[124] The railroad passing through Piedmont did those farmers no good for moving their crop to the mill. Many cotton mills followed along the Dixie Highway outside Greenville around the turn of the century, including Riegel in Ware Shoals and Greenwood Manufacturing in Greenwood.

THE PEOPLE AND THE POLITICS

An Upstate U.S. senator from 1903 to 1908, Asbury Churchill Latimer was a plantation owner near Belton in Anderson County (nine miles from the Augusta Road and within one mile of a railroad station) who worked strategically to promote good roads for farm-to-market availability. He earned his nickname of "Good Roads" Latimer after securing—against great opposition—a favorable report on the need for federal assistance to improve rural public roads. Latimer hoped to create a model system of transportation to help farmers haul products to market.[125] Several initiatives were used over the years to improve road funding in South Carolina.

One early incentive came when Congress inaugurated Rural Free Delivery in 1896 and began building an extensive series of post roads. When the Post Office Department prohibited construction of these roads where existing roads were unfit, farmers got out in force to improve the roads to their properties.[126] In 1904, Latimer proposed a bill for the federal government to supply $24 million in matching funds grants to states to help fund these good roads. The bill provided background and support to the argument of the Congress's ability to support road work in the individual states, but Latimer failed to get it passed before his death in 1908.[127]

C. T. 13—Textile Hall, Greenville, S. C.

Greenville's Textile Hall was home of the Southern Textile Exposition during the first half of the 1900s, when Greenville was considered the Textile Capital of the World.

Senator John Hollis Bankhead of Alabama took the reins in this effort and by World War I was gaining substantial support. Named for him, the Bankhead Highway (U.S. 29) goes through Greenville, South Carolina, as well, and shares the same path as the Dixie Highway through downtown. Designated in 1916, the Bankhead Highway led travelers from Washington, D.C., to San Diego, California. The 1923 National Convention of the Good Roads Association and the Bankhead Highway Association met in Greenville's Textile Hall during the height of Good Roads concerns.[128]

With these two national roads passing through the Upstate, much effort was exerted by the Greenville Chamber of Commerce to pave roads from the center of town as spokes of a wheel during the 1920s. As with the later Dixie Highway plan, various routes for the Bankhead were noted. In the year 1923, the Rand-McNally map showed the Bankhead leaving Greenville with the route down Highway 20 through Piedmont, Pelzer, Williamston and Belton to Anderson. The Bankhead Association map designated a route down Highway 8 to Anderson, bypassing the cotton mill towns. The chamber's journal of the year 1923 states that the Bankhead crossed two other significant highways, the Dixie and the Piedmont, and they planned to pave as much of U.S. 29 (the Bankhead) as possible in the following year. The Piedmont Highway had been paved earlier for better access to the mills along the Saluda River.[129]

FARMING IN TRANSITION

Even with several protracted natural disasters, including floods, then World War I and the 1918 flu, farming was beginning to move into a transition phase along with industry and commerce around the turn of the twentieth century. Cotton fields were devastated by the boll weevil in the 1910s and 1920s, which affected manufacturing. Then, along came the 1929 stock market crash and the Great Depression.

For years, farmers had depended on draft animals for the hard labor—oxen at first and then mules. The mule, a hybrid of a jackass and a mare, was brought to the United States from England and Spain initially. Producing this hybrid was a cumbersome task. President Washington and later Henry Clay were promoters of the use of the mule in farming. Considered progressive, Clay led the early breeding of mules in the United

Farming was in transition in the early twentieth century and mule trade was declining, but so was the small farm. *Clemson University Digital Collections—Cooperative Extension Photographs.*

States, so Kentucky, his home state, became a large producer of these hybrids. The production and use of the mule in farming began an industry in their trade.

Since breeding was never seriously taken up in the Carolinas, mules were some of the animals brought down the Buncombe Turnpike and Augusta Road to Hamburg or Augusta and then dispersed across the South. These work animals plowed cotton fields, pulled wagons and took farm products to market. They were expensive but were the best animal for all kinds of farming tasks in the nineteenth century. Some good breeding animals and mules brought thousands of dollars even at that time. Fortunes were made by breeders, sellers and farmers dealing in mules.[130]

As farming became mechanized and the good roads for truck travel became more important, plantation owners joined the push to promote better, weather-resistant roads. The tractors designed to replace the draft mule were produced in the North, and mule trade declined. This brought about other unforeseen changes across the Southeast. As mule trade lagged, so did driving other trade animals along the Buncombe/Augusta Road. As the mule slowly went out of use, the South saw a decrease in the numbers of farms as well, because many small farmers could not afford tractors. Farmers had been feeding drovers and their animals as a farming sideline, and that money disappeared, too.[131]

The 1950s brought on a decrease in the production of cotton and a move toward people living in the towns. Cities grew. Cotton manufacturing also began to decline, and mills began closing. With this decline in farming, other commerce was needed to fill that void. It came along slowly.[132]

Chapter 6

THE DIXIE HIGHWAY

A Plan to Bring Prosperity to All

Dixie Highway Plan

The Dixie Highway was initially conceived of in 1914 by Carl Fisher, a northern promoter who staged outrageous publicity stunts. One such stunt was pushing a Stoddard off the roof of a building to demonstrate its sturdy construction, although the car was actually made to order specifically for this purpose. He planned cross-country road races and even floated a vehicle and himself over Indianapolis attached to a hot air balloon. Promoting the use of the automobile for long-distance travel from Michigan to Miami, Florida, was a natural extension of his previous work.[133] In April 1915, he and the governors of the states along the proposed Dixie Highway route met in Chattanooga, Tennessee, to form an association to oversee the project, and the Dixie Highway Association was founded.[134]

Passing on to Florida, the Dixie Highway was the way to another of Carl Fisher's schemes: land development. Fisher's Dixie Highway project began pulling automobile magnates and politicians into the project and increasing his wealth by buying and selling the sunny South, Palm Beach specifically.[135] But the early 1925 Florida land boom was bust by 1928 after the Great Miami Hurricane in the fall of 1926 and the Lake Okeechobee Hurricane of September 16, 1928. So, the Great Depression came early to south Florida,[136] leaving the rest of the South to pick up the gauntlet. As many developers of Palm Beach fled back to their northern homes,[137] the

The Dixie Highway map. *Wikipedia.*

branch that was the Dixie Highway passing through the Carolinas continued to be promoted by local automobile associations using the vision of the old South that travelers relished and providing the needed accommodations to make the trip enticing. Motor courts and restaurants popped up along the roadside and provided a greater ease of travel for whites.

African Americans found that the new paved roads enabled them to take advantage of the automobile to travel to the North, Midwest and West. The Great Migration of these families from the South began in the 1910s and continued through the 1950s and 1960s, and Black Americans began looking for jobs and upward mobility or middle-class lifestyles to which the Dixie Highway led. They were slowly becoming able to choose where and when they would like to travel in their own vehicles. The automobile became their armament, "challenging prohibitions [of Jim Crow laws] that prevented them from moving, and they began to claim their rights of citizenship."[138]

After migrating north, musicians and business travelers of color needed the same types of amenities that had grown up along the roads for whites such as overnight accommodations, restaurants, gas stations, garages and occasionally hospitals. During segregation, such necessities were hard to come by for them. A yearly visit back home to see family became a custom for most, and some began to take the road trip to see the United States that became popular after World War II.[139]

Several travel guides for African Americans were produced during this time, but the most thorough and ever popular was *The Negro Motorist Green Book*, which was published from the late 1930s through the 1960s.[140] This guide aided in the motorist's plan for finding necessities along the road. In the 1938 *Green Guide*, there are no entries found in South Carolina or North

Above: A Model T climbs the Saluda Gap on the Dixie Highway prior to 1928 when the road was paved with all-weather concrete.

Left: The focus of the early advertising for the Dixie Highway was Palm Beach, Florida, in the 1910s and 1920s.

The Dixie Highway plan was to bring visitors to Florida from the upper Midwest to sell real estate. *Want to buy some property in Florida?* became a slogan or joke in the 1950s when agents were selling swampland at high prices.

Carolina along U.S. 25, but by the 1947 guide, Augusta, Georgia; Aiken and Greenville, South Carolina; and Asheville, North Carolina, each recorded at least one hotel or tourist home available. Asheville and Greenville had hotels, tourists' homes, restaurants, beauty parlors and barbershops.[141] Greenville even boasted an early hospital and a boardinghouse for musicians in the downtown area. During this time, boardinghouses were popular for Blacks and whites, often providing a business for a widow with empty rooms who supplied some of the best home cooking in the area.[142]

DIXIE HIGHWAY CAROLINA DIVISION

The South needed another boost. So, the idea that these concrete roads would bring commerce and provide consistently usable pathways for farm-to-market, travel and schooling stimulated interest. A period of excitement followed as towns and cities and even historic sites vied for the corridor to pass their way.[143] Textiles and other industries had been growing throughout western South Carolina as part of rebuilding after Reconstruction, and automobiles and trucks were traveling the mud paths that wagon wheels had marked.[144] South Carolina participated in the Good Roads Movement in Columbia with clay and sand-based pack[145] and in the Upstate by improving the Buncombe Road from Greenville north toward Travelers Rest about 1910[146] and then putting down macadam south of Greenville along Augusta Street in about 1912.[147] To continue this work, South Carolina allied with North Carolina to lobby for the modern motorway to cross the mountains onto the Buncombe Turnpike and the Buncombe/Augusta Road, both of which had already been major trade paths, post roads and excursion routes for over one hundred years.[148]

Textile and political leaders in the Upstate also led the Good Roads Movement in the western and northern part of the state. The concrete roads were so important to Upstate mill executives that they exerted much effort and political pressure to make the roads the best possible for movement of cotton to mills. The western corridor from North Carolina to Georgia had long supported commerce and travel from Hamburg (North Augusta) to Hendersonville and had brought textile industry up from Graniteville, the first major cotton mill in the South in the 1840s. Near the Augusta Road, small cotton mills had come and gone.

But after the War Between the States, the success of Piedmont Manufacturing Company funded by Greenville magnates like Vardry McBee flourished and

Morley's Court Motel in Hendersonville, North Carolina, advertises cool summers and springlike winters for a Floridian's paradise and a northerner's playground in the Land of the Sky.

Collins Motor Court
U. S. 25 - 2 MILES NORTH OF GREENVILLE, S. C.

Collins Motor Court was two miles north of Greenville, South Carolina, on U.S. 25 and was billed as having twenty-four modern rooms with private tile baths.

led to the establishment of many mills in the Upstate and North Carolina, especially in Greenville. Brothers W.G. and J.E. Sirrine also led many changes in Greenville. William, a lawyer, pushed hard for the good roads needed in this textile town by forming the Greenville-Hendersonville Highway Association and helping his brother Joe, a noted textile engineer, organize the Southern Textile Exposition in 1913. This biannual meeting brought travelers to the Textile Capital for over forty years.[149] These businessmen, among others, led the New South movement, which fed the growth of industry and the need for the Good Road concrete highway. The routing contest, which was part of the Dixie Highway Association plan, brought heated competition among neighboring routes from north to south. The Carolinas' efforts brought success in 1918.

Designated the Eastern Carolina Division on June 18, 1918,[150] the highway was to enter North Carolina near Hot Springs and travel along the French Broad to Asheville, Hendersonville and Flat Rock. It moved into South Carolina just below Tuxedo, North Carolina, and followed the old trader's path to Merrittsville, Travelers Rest, Greenville, Moonville, Ware Place and Princeton in Greenville County. Through Laurens County, it passed into the new mill town of Ware Shoals, then along to Hodges and Greenwood, next into Edgefield County through that historic town. It passed the Pine House on the eastern road and finally reached the old

The Dixie Court

Located One Mile South of
City Limits on U. S. No. 1 and 78
Augusta, Ga.

Motor courts such as this one south of Augusta, Georgia, were common early accommodations along the road to Florida. (I stayed in one such as this in 2002 outside Bryce Canyon, Utah. Only a bathroom had been added probably in the 1950s. It was surrounded by run-down house trailers with dogs tied under them too.)

site of Hamburg in the current town of North Augusta before crossing the Savannah River into Augusta, Georgia. This path initially led through dirt roads in the countryside and some paved roads in cities and towns. The actual paving took over a decade to complete.

Chapter 7

PAVING THE ROAD POLITICS

The Issues

T he need to pave the dirt roadways in a more stable, weather-resistant material was evident to most Carolinians by the 1910s. Automobile travel had become a passion across the nation, and even accounting for all the issues to laying concrete, that was exactly what seemed to be coming. Automobiling and driving clothing and accessories were the rage, even if you did not own a vehicle. To take a driving excursion in a car with no doors, windshield or top, riders needed protection from the elements of weather and dust and mud from the dirt roads. Driving and riding attire of all kinds became common. Doctors recommended washing out the eyes after a ride even if goggles were worn. Although the coats worn in the North were heavy leather or fur styles, in the South, more lightweight dusters were the most practical. By the 1920s, these styles were fading as the vehicles began to be enclosed and roads were beginning to be paved.[151]

DISTILLATION

At this point, Greenville was moving toward becoming the Textile Center of the World, so transporting goods to and from the Upstate became paramount. Textile and political leaders in the area participated in conferences with the Dixie Highway Association based in Chattanooga, Tennessee, and with cohorts in Asheville, North Carolina, to make the

This page: The times were changing when this image of the John Tollett and Robert West family was taken in about 1894. John is proud of his horses, but Robert was sporting automobiling attire with goggles. The vehicle can barely be seen on the right of the photograph. The motoring glasses are part of the Piedmont Historical Collection in the Piedmont Museum.

The red Model T is now on the Dixie Highway between Asheville and Hendersonville, North Carolina. This section of the road looks slightly better than the gap road it was on earlier.

Eastern Carolina Division happen.[152] Since the Dixie Highway was coming down from the northern part of the country, the road from Asheville was a key component of commerce and travel. That path had always been down the Saluda Gap into the northeast corner of Greenville County, which was often referred to as the Dark Corner.

The boosters of the New South in Greenville considered the liquor-producing folks of the Dark Corner as backward and hostile, so this part of the Dixie Highway was problematic for them. Even as Prohibition and temperance movements took over the country in the 1920s, the backcountry Appalachians there continued their distillation and related confrontations with law enforcement, the revenuers. The boosters of Greenville's New South even considered the Dark Corner as seceded from the county, and they attempted to hide news of the area from the national papers.[153]

The Dark Corner was politically and economically disassociated from the rest of Greenville County and the state and had been so even in the antebellum period. The area's physical isolation from the rest of South Carolina exacerbated and magnified the political and social tendencies it shared with its Appalachian neighbors. The geography of the area did not allow productive growth of cotton, as did the terrain of the rest of the county or state. Therefore, economic opportunities were limited to subsistence

Above: Two men famous in the craft distillery process, Troy Cagle and Popcorn Sutton, display their wares in front of their typical running vehicles from back in the day.

Left: An anonymous Appalachian moonshiner posed for this picture in the 1950s.

farming and home distillation. This left the mountainous areas of Greenville to be the lowest-income-producing portions of the county. Many of these families moved into the textile villages around Greenville to find work with consistent pay. The cotton farmers of the rest of the county supported efforts to defend the cotton economy, but the Dark Corner farmers basically grew cabbage, corn, wheat and only enough cotton for home use in their rich river bottoms. With the bulky bushels of corn being an issue for transportation to market in Greenville or Asheville, especially on muddy mountain roads, farmers were forced to look for other means of using their produce. Distilling alcohol was a viable option and became a prevalent product.[154]

Legal production of alcohol was part of commerce in the Dark Corner following the War Between the States, but government distilleries were required to pay a tax. Most local producers chose not to pay, and revenuers attempted to collect the tax or arrest the offenders. This work collecting the taxes entailed traveling from Greenville to the mountains, and the revenuers often ignored the products unless there was a complaint, which often came from other makers who would receive a reward for providing a still's location.[155] During Prohibition, the Dixie Highway earned monikers like "Avenue de Booze" and "Rummers' Runway" as spirits were transported from Canada into the South, but the Dark Corner had been trafficking for

White lightnin', moonshine, the critter—all have been names for the corn liquor produced in the Dark Corner of Greenville County, South Carolina.

decades. Gun battles with law enforcement officers and rival families were notorious. Death was almost an accepted part of the distillation process.[156]

As the better roads brought travelers from across the states, the Corner became less dark because mountain folks gained an understanding of other Americans and even travelers from other counties of the state.[157] For instance, in nearby Spartanburg County, Camp Wadsworth, a World War I army training camp, affected the Dark Corner's isolation. Troops came into Greenville County daily and fired live artillery into Hogback Mountain. Locals welcomed these soldiers for various reasons. Mainly, farmers were able to sell more moonshine, and their wives sold food and other homemade goods to the young men who were far away from their own homes.[158] After the war, the Dixie Highway brought travelers down the Saluda Gap into the Upstate mountains and continued the mix of the cultures, but distillation in the Dark Corner continued into the 1960s and early 1970s at least. The Corner did not completely lose its violent reputation until late in the twentieth century. These issues may be a contributing factor in why paving this section of the national highway was significantly delayed. In the 1980s and 1990s, high-end housing developments took over Glassy Mountain and surrounding areas and have brought even greater diversity to the Corner.[159]

OTHER TENSIONS

The initial plan to move northerners to Miami was based on the sale of the automobile and moving farm products to market. Farmers and automobile magnates became the major interests in the Good Roads Movement, and they crafted the plans for the named roads and marked trails. After the initial announcement of the Dixie Highway plan, the Dixie Highway Association formed an alliance of stakeholders like auto makers, civic supporters, local road officials, farmers and other concerned citizens to promote a competition for the routing of the thoroughfare. This competition set locals against locals and town against town but started the promotion of the road.[160]

The Carolina Division Highway was viewed as key to commerce in lower realms of the route, but the work did not proceed fast enough. North Augusta, in a corner of Aiken County, was not linked to Edgefield as quickly as the land speculators there would have liked. In July 1927, the mayor of North Augusta, Dr. Robert Mealing, threatened Aiken County with secession if a good paved road was not immediately built, and he

The Flanders "20" Glidden Pathfinder passing a cane mill along the "Dixie Trail." Two mule-power suffices to cut the cane and squeeze out the juice for molasses

Road races on the Dixie Trail were popular since the roads were not crowded. Often beginning the race in New England or the Midwest, racers usually did not complete the run. This Flanders "20" was the lowest-priced car in the Glidden Tour from New York City to Jacksonville in 1911, and it finished the race even through the slippery red clay of the Carolinas was only surpassed in "cussedness" by the shifting sands of Florida.

TAKING THE HURDLES IN THE HITCHCOCK WOODS

POLO WHITNEY FIELD

AIKEN, S. C.

Queen of Winter Resorts

Pure Water
Dry Climate
The
Winter Playground
of the South

FERMATA SCHOOL

116834

Aiken is still the Queen of Winter Resorts for the horse culture.

called for a mass council meeting with members of the Edgefield citizenry to proceed with this objective. Edgefield citizen representatives stated that unless action was soon taken by Aiken to pave the main highway through North Augusta, they would ask for annexation into Edgefield County. Both towns agreed that the road was the natural connecting link between the area and the rest of South Carolina.[161] This secession did not come about, but it shows the contention that good roads caused across the length of the Dixie Highway and the possible delay of the needed bridge construction over the Savannah River.

The process of the construction of the Dixie Highway helped move the country toward the beginning of the federal government's monetary and legal support of transcontinental vehicular transportation. It became a template for a government-funded interstate highway system through many heated debates crafting ideological and political legacies that would later be realized in a presidential plan.

THE MILITARY

As World War I moved into the realm of possibility, military concerns came to the forefront of thought, and the Dixie Highway Association was able to garner government support for a good interstate highway system. This brought two military camps into the Upstate: Camp Sevier near Greenville and, in Spartanburg County, Camp Wadsworth near the Dark Corner, both positively affecting the local economy. The Dixie Highway Association refocused its campaign to incorporate fast movement of soldiers and equipment to trains and waterways.

Deliberations of the necessity of good roads for military purposes caused debates over the funding of roadways, which had always been paid for locally by private individuals investing in toll roads and bridges. For almost one hundred years, locals had been required to maintain their own roads or pay to have it done. Even after 1900, rural areas continued this process. Silas Trowbridge of Piedmont recorded in his notes in 1904 that he was paying for three days of road work clearing ditches and building up creek banks with several men and a team.[162] During the 1800s, the state had given the right to build roads and bridges to individuals or groups who then were allowed to charge tolls for their use. These had always been private ventures, and the builder was required to maintain the road or bridge ongoing. Following

Above: This street on Vanderbilt Road to North Carolina from Camp Wadsworth was in Spartanburg, South Carolina, during World War I. Soldiers from this camp came into the Dark Corner of Greenville County to practice shooting munitions into Hog Back Mountain, providing the hill folks with another venue for selling their wares. *Veterans Voices website.*

Left: Farmer Silas Trowbridge of Piedmont recorded in his notebook all the money he spent in 1904. Here he noted the twelve-dollar cost for cleaning out ditches and paying a team and several men to build up creek banks. All of this is part of his road maintenance requirement. *Greenville County Library, Trowbridge Collection.*

Reconstruction, wealthy constituents were allowed to hire a chain gang crew to work on personal projects. The counties' general lack of oversight of these crews promoted graft and abuse and continuing resentment and suspicion.[163] Often, African Americans were arrested just to add to the chain gang's productivity.[164] Finally, military use of the roads threw the costs of maintenance into the purview of the federal government.

FUNDING

Everyone wanted the weatherproof good roads, and working out these transportation issues brought about changes in the South. The progressives felt these concrete roads supported the betterment of life for all. The cotton industry grew through improved agricultural practices related to cotton production, especially the tractor. Good roads provided new vacation and travel-related businesses. Education for all was encouraged by allowing the consolidation of school systems along these usable roads. Commercial trucking routes increased, and armies moved quickly across the country during war times.[165] No matter how necessary good roads were, creating these roads was still a struggle.

At the beginning of the 1900s, the push moved to the states and the federal government to provide good roads for more national interests. Senator "Good Roads" Latimer had pushed for federal funding, realizing that the states could not manage total support. Although farmers wanted the good roads, they didn't want to be taxed for them and, therefore, would block taxation with their votes.[166] Finding means of funding the paving of the roads had been a political issue for decades. Many Carolinians feared corruption in local, county and state government when large amounts of tax money were doled out. Some felt that forming departments of transportation in counties and the state would allow corruption to prevail and that giving the state power over the maintenance and building of roads would promote nepotism, favoritism and graft. Farmers especially were reluctant to provide monetary support for work they could easily complete with their own crews.

North Carolina's N. Buckner, heading the Western Carolina Motor Club, worked to circumvent many issues by using the club's funds to support paving in North Carolina and the states just north. In South Carolina, most of the issues were related to raising the funds for road construction across the state.

A young man working the roads.

Convincing the voters to approve road bonds and taxes was challenging. People who felt motivated about the roads during the winter forgot about it during summer and voted against funding in the fall.[167] Articles across the state promoted paving with concrete over asphalt/macadam by using examples from northern and midwestern roads and comparing costs.[168] Although generally accepted as the best surface material, the cost of a concrete road was substantial, and with the probability of graft and nepotism high, locals found numerous reasons to continue to vote down funding sources.[169]

Greenville County's state legislators had all been elected on a good roads platform and moved forward in 1915 to bond the county. They passed a bond act for $950,000 for paving and did so without a referendum. The courts upheld, and work proceeded. Soon, other counties in the Upstate and later across the state followed suit. Greenville's road-building program set the mark for the state, but even the Buncombe/Augusta Road wasn't completed into North Carolina until at least 1928.

In 1917, South Carolina formed the State Highway Commission to study methods of scientific road engineering and to advise and assist the counties, but the department soon acquired the building and maintenance of miles and miles of intrastate roads.[170] Also, the Rhett Plan for building roads was promoted by the South Carolina Automobile Association in 1918, and it was presented as a bill to the legislature in 1919. This plan required $25 million to be appropriated, and its impetus was the support from the Automobile Association, which had grown from zero members to thousands in a year. This option was for taxation of automobile owners through tags and bonds to be paid by increased taxation on the vehicles.[171] These efforts were a beginning, but little success was available until after at least another decade of struggle to find consistent funding.

Chapter 8

ACTUALLY PAVING THE ROAD

CONSTRUCTION

Even as a dirt road, the Dixie Highway was one of the first interstate highways in the Carolinas and one of the first in the nation. It became United States Highway 25 in 1926 when the federal government first established these roads for the benefit of the whole nation, not just the individual states. This concrete Dixie Highway System became the backbone of the new interstate road system and then became a casualty of its own success. It had been in existence for less than ten years. By the late 1920s, the red-and-white Dixie Highway signs began disappearing from most roadways, although it was still referred to as the Dixie Highway in many areas of western Carolina.[172]

Not all of U.S. Highway 25 was paved initially. Paving moved outward from the centers of the cities. In Greenville County, the northernmost section through the Dark Corner and Saluda Gap was one of the last to be paved. The section from Edgefield to North Augusta was also one of the hardest to construct, with delays prompting North Augusta to threaten to secede from Aiken County into Edgefield unless construction began immediately.[173] The Jefferson Davis Bridge over the Savannah River in North Augusta was a necessary part of the Carolina Division of the Dixie Highway but was not actually built until 1931, well after the demise of the Dixie Highway Association. The actual construction outside the cities began in 1927 and

Road construction at Camp Wadsworth. *South Carolina Digital Library—Road Work.*

ended in 1931 with the construction of the Jefferson Davis Memorial Bridge over the Savannah River as part of U.S. Highway 25.[174]

Support for the Dixie Highway paving project was generally widespread as the project moved forward in late 1928. The *Greenville News* stated, "Paving the Dixie is one of the most important matters to South Carolina and all the states on that route….The Dixie highway traverses approximately 145 miles of South Carolina soil….The improvement of this highway will be of tremendous local as well as national benefit."[175]

NORTH CAROLINA

Leading the way for the paving of the Dixie Highway in North Carolina was N. Buckner, an energetic citizen who served as a member of the Dixie Highway Association and the director of the Western Carolina Motor Club. He worked with groups in Tennessee and South Carolina to link the roads to support tourist flow from north to south. Advertising the Carolina Route, Buckner's association placed road signs directing tourists to the route even into Florida and published maps that were distributed into the northern and southern states. Even prior to the completion of paving, 150 to 200 vehicles a day were traveling from Tennessee through the Carolinas to Florida on this "shortcut to the sea."[176] Buckner and A. Cothran of Greenville formed an alliance to aid in the progress. With oversight from Buckner, the Automobile Association provided funds and engineering to the states of Tennessee and Kentucky to begin their work. With this support, locals in both of those states stepped forward, supplying materials and labor at greatly reduced rates to build a stable roadbed leading to North Carolina. At that time, the Buncombe Turnpike was the only road connecting North Carolina and Tennessee.[177]

In 1921, the North Carolina General Assembly issued a $50 million bond to be paid by a license fee and a one-cent-per-gallon gasoline tax. In 1931, it also accepted the maintenance of the highways, which the Depression forced. Asheville began paving downtown streets and boasted having 220 miles of hard surface roads by 1924.[178]

SOUTH CAROLINA

One section of the highway in southern Greenville County was twenty-two miles. Being the longest section and on a ridge, the contract was given to one company with a masterful plan for completion of the task. Claussen-Lawrence Construction Company from Augusta, Georgia, proposed to move materials along the way using an industrial small track railroad system that would be portable. The track began at the end of the concrete four miles south of the town in Gantt and then followed the roadbed to Princeton at the Laurens County line. This contract was for the longest road mileage of any contract in South Carolina at the time. The road builders loaded the materials to "batch boxes," which were pulled along the narrow-gauge industrial line to where they were needed. At that point, the batch boxes were lifted by crane and their contents emptied into mixers.[179] This work was completed during the fall and winter of 1927–28. As a child, Ben Knight's father, Allen, roller skated on the new road in the southern part of Greenville County.[180]

The paving of U.S. 25 north of Greenville was also taking place in 1927 and 1928. During the construction, this mountainous section was rerouted across an old section of the State Road crossing the 1820 Poinsett Bridge as a temporary detour for traffic. The Greenville Watershed now covers most of this land, and the earliest sections of the State Road are inaccessible to the public.

It wasn't until 1929 that the South Carolina legislature finally passed the state highway bond act providing $65 million to complete the construction of the highway systems. This event sounded the death knell of county lines and local viewpoints in the matter of constructing highways. "May 20, 1930—the date of the first letting under the state highway bond act—will stand always as a landmark in the material progress of the state," Ben Sawyer, chief commissioner of the South Carolina Department of Transportation, stated in the *Charlotte Observer*.[181] Sawyer started as chief in 1926, and historian David Wallace felt that Sawyer, "with economy and efficiency," constructed the state's modern roads in spite of political wrangling by governors.[182] This money was available for the construction of the bridges at the Savannah River on the Dixie Highway in 1931.

NATIONAL

Convincing the federal government to supply funds for these concrete roads was seen as necessary, which was a drastic change in philosophy across the country, including the Carolinas. States' rights had been paramount in the thinking of Carolinians of all economic situations. But as the South dealt with Jim Crow laws disenfranchising African Americans for decades and progressive concerns that all citizens should be provided opportunities for

T.C. Gower created this Street Sweeper, circa 1910. One of Greenville's cotton mills is in the background. *Greenville County Library Collection.*

jobs and education, progressive leaders began to see the federal government as a link to support basic needs for all Americans. Later, as the Depression worsened in the 1930s and the Works Progress Administration put folks to work in various improvement projects, money was funneled into the paving of the National Highway System through these state roads commissions. By 1932, the three north–south running federal interstate highways in South Carolina—the Dixie Highway (U.S. 25), the Capital Highway (U.S. 1) and the Atlantic Coastal Highway (U.S. 17)—had become uniformly paved, all-weather throughways.[183]

The Dixie Highway experiment came to an end over controversy brought about by these difficulties, but this hard, contentious process of growth led to economic prosperity as improved transportation increased traffic through the Carolinas.

Chapter 9

THE NEW MODERN SOUTH

The Eisenhower Connection

Long-Term Benefits

The Dixie Highway/U.S. 25 bridges in North Augusta were finally finished in 1931, completing the road long fought for in the Carolinas. In 1939, the Federal Writers' Project working in South Carolina compiled a state guide. At that point, every county was linked by paved roads and "hardly a place in the State was more than six miles from a paved road." From this we know that the concrete road, being paved between 1927 and 1931, would have been a significant early road.[184]

Travel

By the 1940s, the Dixie Highway was nearly forgotten, and its place in building the modern society of the South and nation was lost to most. But travel was again a boost to the Carolina economy, as it had been with the Lowcountry visitors in the 1800s. This Dixie Highway Progressive-era project brought northerners from the Midwest to the sunny South and put money in the pockets of the property owners along the route. Some of those travelers visited and then decided to stay, as did Ray Whitney and his family in 1936.

Coming from Ohio, the Whitneys settled at a wide place on the road in southern Greenville County then called Woodville. They purchased the home where Dr. Woodside and his wife, Ellen, parents of the Greenville textile magnates the Woodside brothers, had lived. They built a motor court, Ohio Home Camp, and ran it from 1936 to 1953. Ray and his wife, Katie, built the ten-cabin camp with their sons. This was the only overnight resting place between Greenville and Greenwood at the time, and it attracted visitors like country music legends Flatt and Scruggs. Later, Ray and Katie left the South Carolina business to their son, Bob, and his family and built a larger motor court in St. Augustine, Florida, also on U.S. 25.

Ice water seems to have been a treat for travelers along roadsides early on. Angie Whitney McDonald, Bob's daughter, remembers taking that soothing drink to visitors at their camp.[185] Wall Drug in Wall, South Dakota, is now a major tourist complex that started by providing ice water to early dust-covered travelers along the main road from Chicago to Portland, Oregon. Road signs, like "See Rock City" across the South, still promote Wall Drug's free ice water.

Other businesses supporting travelers profited—gas stations for one. At that time, stations had attendants pumping gas, washing windows and checking oil. One Moonville attendant, Pete Peden, remembered servicing a family on the road to Florida and giving them advice about where to eat along the way. In about three hours, the same car returned for more gas. Everyone realized that the family had traveled south to the restaurant, and after eating, when they left the parking lot, they turned north instead of south. They didn't recognize anything until they saw the filling station again.[186]

MILITARY

Another continuing effect of early roads in Greenville was the military aspect. Because of warmer southern winters, several camps were part of training grounds for year-round use, including Camp Wetherill in downtown Greenville during the Spanish-American War (1898–99) and Camp Sevier during World War I along the northern part of the city. The roads provided good access for the thousands of military men, nurses and officers who came with trains of wagons loaded with supplies.[187] These encampments also brought new commercial ventures leading to a new prosperity, and the city fathers remembered this as World War II loomed. Reaching out

Donaldson Army Air Base aircraft hangars, circa 1982. *Collection of Bob Dicey.*

to Washington in the early 1940s, these leaders were successful in bringing to the area the Greenville Army Air Base, covering two thousand acres south of town. This new group of soldiers and the construction of airplane runways enabled the area to turn the base into an ongoing industrial draw when it closed in the 1960s.[188] The Buncombe/Augusta Road converging in Greenville County with the State Road and the Bankhead Highway, often called the Super Highway, has provided the best of good roads for continued industrial growth.

Eisenhower's Interstate Highways

In the 1950s, a new president, who had seen the necessity of good roads for military transports across the South and West during World War I, came into office and implemented another good transportation idea. An experiment in 1917 by the Dixie Highway Association proved the significantly increased speed of movement along the concrete Dixie Highway by the military from Atlanta to Chattanooga. A particular young officer was serving there at the time. In 1919, that same young officer, Dwight Eisenhower, also participated in an arduous transcontinental military caravan experiment crossing the country from the upper Midwest to the Pacific.

This page: These road signs were seen along U.S. 25 sometime during its history. The Dixie Highway Map cover advertises the Blue Ridge Mountain route through North and South Carolina, circa 1950. *Strom Thurmond Institute, Clemson University (Dixie Highway Association, Corbin, Kentucky), authors' collection and Wikipedia.*

Convinced of the need for weatherproof, long-distance highways, especially in wartime, President and General Eisenhower moved to ensure these roadways would be constructed, and quickly. The Dwight D. Eisenhower National Interstate and Defense Highways Act was signed into law on June 29, 1956.[189] For the Carolinas, this law brought several major thoroughfares: I-95 from Maine to Florida; I-26/40/75 from the Upper Peninsula of Michigan to Charleston; I-20 from I-95 to Texas; and I-85 from Richmond, Virginia, to Montgomery, Alabama. For North Carolina, I-40 transports travelers across the country to California. These roads move interstate commerce and defense supplies and people rapidly throughout the United States, but the older United States highways, like U.S. 25, continue to support local towns and rural areas not serviced by Eisenhower's limited-access thoroughfares.

NEW SOUTH

During the years from 1915 to 1925, the modern South, urban portions of the Carolinas and the Carolinas' western ridge were defined mainly through the transportation issues that arose from the construction of the Dixie Highway, issues that in 1926 led to the changing of federal roads such as the Dixie Highway into U.S. Highway 25. Into the 1930s and 1940s, the federal road system veiled the red-and-white DH signage, and

Evidence of an abandoned concrete road where weeds grow in the expansion joints.

the Dixie Highway became a forgotten title, but the long-term effects of the process of building the concrete road across the states forged the foundations needed to create transportation efforts for the future.[190]

Twelve sections of this extant concrete from the original Dixie Highway/ U.S. 25 have been identified in Henderson County of North Carolina and Greenville, Edgefield and Aiken Counties of South Carolina. One section in Henderson County, near Fletcher, was left when a marshy area of the road was rerouted. In Greenville, these sections were bypassed by new construction over the years. In Edgefield County, the portions of concrete are related to bridge construction sites. For Aiken County, which has a short section of the concrete road, the known extant sections are two bridges with a small park between them. Those remnants remind us that the Dixie Highway/U.S. 25 initiative was the foundation of all our interstate highways today and that those roads were the ways to a modern South and a more prosperous nation.

CONCLUSION

In his text *Dirt Roads to Dixie*, Howard Preston argues that the main factor in the construction of all-weather roads in the 1920s and early 1930s was the massive increase in the numbers of automobiles owned by the emerging middle class across the country. With this in mind, the early paved road was simply forced into existence by the rapidly growing automotive industry. Alternatively, Tammy Ingram suggests in *Dixie Highway* that several movements came together in the early twentieth century—efforts that led to a modern America. With various groups including farmers, educators, store owners, politicians, industrialists and developers jumping on the same bandwagon, the best of the best found ways to bring their constituents to the bar and improve the situations of most. The federal government's ability and willingness to provide support to the states finally became an acceptable means.

Farmers had better farm-to-market roads, politicians were able to get their constituents to agree on something and, although Miami wasn't the pearl developers expected initially, they were able to promote hotels and motels along the byways. Even the minority populations took the good roads to leave the poor southern farms for the northern industrial cities to find a middle-class lifestyle. Students rode to school more quickly, and education for most became a reality. A good job for the majority was an outcome that moved this agrarian country to a modern industrial nation after World War II.

It seems most logical, then, that Ingram's broad theory, which includes the growth of the automobile's use across the country by the rich and middle classes, also shows connections to the Progressive New South and the industrialization of the country. These movements converged, allowing the connections to be accomplished and U.S. Highway 25 to be completed.

The importance of this trail, the Augusta Road and the Buncombe Turnpike (1766–68), is in the realm of several trails in the history of the United States. Some famous early trails—the King's Highway (1650–1735), the Santa Fe Trail (1822) and the Oregon Trail (1811–40)—have been duly noted in the history books. Though not as long, this Carolina trace evidences communication like the King's Highway, trade like the Santa Fe Trail and, like the Oregon Trail, it shares the westward expansion and brave movement of pioneers searching for a better life. Furthermore, this road contributed to the industrialization of the South through the textile industry and the participation in the Good Roads Movement leading to the Modern New South. It also relates the good, the bad and the ugly of the process of development of this union of immigrants from colonization through today and into the future. Therefore, this drover's road and interstate highway should be studied and listed with the oldest and most historic trails in this country. The time is overdue to recognize, study and share.

PART III

FOR YOUR TRAVELS

"Stomping" with the authors on the concrete road.

Chapter 10

ON THE ROAD AGAIN

The Dirt and the Concrete

THE DIRT: EXTANT SITES

The dirt roads were bison trails, Indian paths and wagon roads and were not anywhere near straight. They followed the easiest route. The following sections of the dirt trail are what we have left as evidence of how hard travel was for our forbearers. Much of this road has been paved, but some of it is visible as deep cuts in the wooded areas along the Carolina roadsides.

- **Hot Springs**: This historic town on the Appalachian Trail is across the French Broad River from the actual drover's road. Off U.S. 25, turn onto River Road and then right when you come to a dead end. Along the French Broad east of Hot Springs is an old section of the Buncombe Turnpike drover's road. It is paved part of the way but turns into a gravel road and then dirt as it moves north toward the Tennessee line. A small state park, Murray Branch Recreation Area, in the Pisgah National Forest has picnic tables and a restroom. Many rental cabins are along this portion of the road, and a small sign designates it as the Buncombe Turnpike. The site of the old iron bridge can be seen at the sign. At this sign, turn left to drive under the current concrete bridge over the river to get to the beginning of the hiking trail to Lover's Leap rock. This attraction can also be

The River Road along the French Broad near Hot Springs, North Carolina. This drover's road is partially black topped, then gravel, then dirt.

seen from the bridge over the river when traveling away from Hot Springs to Walnut.

The drover's road from Hot Springs followed the French Broad River to the little town of Marshall, which is just off the current U.S. 25. Now, the old drover's road can be accessed by getting to the French Broad Parkway.

- **Walnut**: Another turn off U.S. 25 is to take the "old road" to Walnut. At the top of the hill is the old church, which was the first courthouse for the county. Enjoy the cemetery and the view from behind the church. Travel to Marshall on U.S. 25 or take Little Pine Road to Redmon Road to pick up the old route. The railroad track leaves Hot Springs from the west side of the river and then crosses it on an iron bridge to travel to Marshall.
- **Marshall**: On the Buncombe Turnpike, Marshall was on the drover's road along the river and is now the seat of Madison County. Set in the beautiful deep French Broad River gorge, the narrow downtown has many historic turn-of-the-twentieth-

Left: View along the River Road near Hot Springs, North Carolina. The River Road was the Buncombe Turnpike in the 1800s and the original drover's road.

Below: View of the French Broad River on River Road, Hot Springs.

Opposite, top left: Cabins for rent along the Buncombe Turnpike, River Road, Hot Springs.

Opposite, top right: A walking trail now leads to Lover's Leap.

Opposite, bottom: View from Walnut, North Carolina, and the old cemetery.

Above: Vintage filling station and cars in downtown Marshall, North Carolina.

century stores, some untouched. Take Old Marshall Highway along the river east, and it turns into Riverside Drive, also known as State Road 251. This drive passes along the river for a number of miles. Note several lovely bridges over creeks and a few crossing the river. As you near Weaverville, don't miss crossing the river to visit the tiny historic town of Craggy with its very old gristmill on the railroad tracks. Return to State Road 251 to Weaverville.

- **Weaverville**: Sitting on a dry ridge just north of Asheville, Weaverville was chartered in 1875 but had been on the Buncombe Turnpike all along. Some pieces of the original road can be found here but have been paved.

In the French Broad River Valley, the railroad passes on the south and the drover's road, now U.S. 25, passes on the north.

- **Asheville**: The Buncombe Turnpike came through downtown Asheville from Weaverville to Pack Square. The direct road is no longer visible. It has been crossed and blocked by I-40 and I-26. But at Pack Square are the sculptures marking the drover's roads that crossed on a hill. From Pack Square, go through Biltmore Village, and from there you may take U.S. 25-A, Sweeten Creek Road, which was the old road. It is the slowest route through residential areas with many lights. If you take U.S. 25 toward Fletcher, you can pick up sections of the old road there.
- **Hendersonville**: From Asheville, take the old road to Hendersonville through Fletcher. Sections of the old road have names starting with "Old." One section is in the fence surrounding a concrete plant. Be careful if you go farther than the concrete plant, as you will encounter a construction company or, in the other direction, a dead end of dirt and gravel. Turning around takes a number of points, not just three. Old Asheville Road is a dirt and gravel section of the old drover's road. Another is Old Brickyard.
- **Flat Rock**: Tracing through the resort of Flat Rock, many mid-century motor courts sit along the road. One of the area's oldest inns, Woodfield, still entertains visitors. Visit poet Carl

The Grove Park Inn opened in 1903 and has served the public for over one hundred years. This Omni Hotel once served the military during World War II. It is open to the public for tours as well.

Historic Woodfield Inn in Flat Rock, North Carolina, was built in 1852 and is in the National Register of Historic Places. Flat Rock was a summer vacation draw for South Carolina's Lowcountry planters during the 1800s.

Sandburg's farm, where descendants of his wife's prize-winning milk goats still enjoy the cool weather. The interior of the home has not been changed; even his office still has his cigars and glasses.

- **Tuxedo**: The drover's road in this state line town can still be seen in broken portions. The road from Flat Rock comes down to Old Greenville Highway and South Lake Summit Road. The Green Cove Community road is near an old iron bridge that points to the dirt road on the mountainside, identified as Bell Mountain Road on aerial maps. It is not very drivable but would make a nice walk.

Take Old U.S. 25 toward South Carolina and note the North Carolina State Historical Marker for the Vance Duel along the right side of the road. At the tree line across the field is the dirt drover's road, and on the other side of Old U.S. 25 is the road named Kingdom Place. This is the area of the Kingdom of Happy Land during the late 1900s (see chapter 11).

View of two bridges in Tuxedo, North Carolina, the borderline town on the drover's road to Augusta, Georgia.

The Saluda Gap starts here as you pass into South Carolina. Parts of the oldest trail are now owned by the Greenville Water System. The Old U.S. 25 runs through the North Saluda Reservoir, where signs are posted about staying in the car. The reservoir is fenced. Please respect the water system's resource.

- **Merrittsville**: This camp on the drover's road was an important rest area for the animals and men in the 1800s. At this town, the South Carolina State Road turned east toward Columbia and the Augusta Road turned west to Greenville. The State Road was built in 1820 by Joel Poinsett, the Mexican ambassador who brought the poinsettia to us for Christmas decorations. The 1820 Poinsett Bridge is near the exit from the reservoir's dam on Callahan Mountain Road. Merrittsville was covered by the reservoir in the early 1960s.
- **Travelers Rest**: The drover's road wove down the mountain and hills, and evidence can still be found at the Goodwin House at the intersection of U.S. 25 and Scenic Highway 11.

View of 1800s farm outbuildings on Callahan Mountain Road off Old U.S. 25 in upper Greenville County, South Carolina.

The Goodwin House was an inn and stage stop on the Buncombe Road in northern Greenville County, South Carolina. It is owned by Greenville County, and the exterior has been restored and the county is looking for funding for the interior work. *Collection of Kyle Campbell.*

This inn was first constructed prior to 1800, and the original hand-hewn logs were uncovered during its recent restoration. If you pass the inn, you can travel Old Settlement Road, which turns off Highway 11 to the south. It comes out on current U.S. 25. Other sections of the old road can be driven on the way to Travelers Rest. Old Buncombe is a good example, but it is paved over.

In Travelers Rest, go through downtown to the bandstand and turn behind the main drag onto Old Buncombe Road. Spring Park Inn just after you turn was on the old trade road and was built in the mid-1800s. Passing on down the way to a pastoral setting is a 1910 concrete bridge.

- **Downtown Greenville**: Follow the Buncombe Road into downtown, passing through mill villages from the early 1900s. The drovers brought the animals through downtown on Main Street. Most of the early buildings were replaced by 1900, but a number from the turn of the century still stand. This Greenville is in the midst of being a popular tourist attraction once again. From Greenville's Main Street, the road turns south to Augusta Street. This connection of Main, Pendleton and Augusta is the beginning of the use of that name for the path. Along the street was Furman College (now University), which has moved to Travelers Rest. Many historic homes can be found along the Augusta Street section in town. Sections of Old Augusta Road that are cutoffs of the current road are scattered throughout the southern part of the county.

- **South Greenville**: Along the old road are many treasures for travelers. From Moonville to Princeton, one hundred houses over one hundred years old still stand, and most are still lived in. See how many you can count. One that needs saving is just south of Moonville, Greenville Memorial Gardens and historic Pepper School. The 1850s plantation house is noted for the steppingstone near the road. It was for mounting a horse or carriage, and the widened road was routed around it. Another of these plantation homes still has a metal hitching post. Along the way is the community of Woodville, where the four Woodside brothers of Woodside Cotton Mills fame grew up; the brick building at the intersection was their bank. At the next intersection, Ware Place (1820) is the home of an extremely wealthy plantation owner, T. Edwin Ware, who was involved in the greatest trial of the century in Greenville County. Near Princeton, another massive plantation is the McCullough House, which is the oldest brick building in the county (1812). This homeplace is soon to be restored by Fork Shoals Historical Society.

The McCullough House in the 1940s
[view from the south]
Note absence of upper and lower piazzas
(from a postcard owned by the McCullough family)

The McCullough House was an inn and stagecoach stop on the Augusta Road in the 1800s. It has been remodeled twice; this image is of the current Colonial Revival façade. A large number of these postcard advertisements were found in the attic by a family member during the late 1900s.

- **To Indian Mound Road**: Moving on south near Ware Shoals, turn left onto Indian Mound Road. This old road does pass an Indian mound visible in a pasture. Turn onto Riverfork Road going toward Lake Greenwood, then turn onto Smith Bridge Road. Here you will come to a dead end because the road went across the Saluda River over the toll Smith Bridge, which is now in Lake Greenwood. The foundation pillars can be seen on aerials in the water near the old Donaldson Air Force Base Recreation Area. The old officers' club is still visible on the south side of Lake Greenwood on Ridge Road. From the current U.S. 25, Ridge Road to the recreation area is dirt and gravel. Signage by the lake explains the Native American path and early trails crossing the river here. Ridge Road goes to State Road 246, passing through Coronaca and on to Ninety Six, where the Revolutionary Star Fort is a National Historic Site.
- **Ninety Six**: A hidden gem of the National Park Service, Ninety Six was a fort in the backcountry shaped like a star. The history of Ninety Six is extensive, and it runs along a railroad track. Cambridge was a town close to the fort with much focus on religion and education, but it has pretty much disappeared. From this area, the trade roads divided. Going to Meeting Street will take you on Old Edgefield Road through dirt forest service roads. To the west, the road went to Kirksey, a pottery village.

The drover's road ruts from Ninety Six to Kirksey are very visible in the woods in the evenings when shadows lay long. Noon hides the deep cuts. Some are also visible on the road toward Cambridge. Put your Google map setting to terrain and the cuts will stand out, showing where to look. Try driving slowly on State Road 248 leaving the Star Fort, then weave to Martin Towne Road looking for the deep cuts along the road. North Martintown Road and Martintown Road bypass Edgefield to the west on the way to Augusta.

At Kirksey, go south toward Edgefield, but stop along the way to see Turkey Creek and the old concrete road U.S. 25. There along the concrete near the abandoned bridge, look to the east to find the deep ruts of the drover's road. Then travel on to Edgefield, past the old Jug Town where enslaved persons crafted stoneware jugs for their masters—jugs that are prized by collectors now.

This extant store on Indian Mound Road along the old drover's trail to Hamburg is near Ware Shoals, South Carolina.

These pylons are evidence of Smith Bridge of the old drover's road to Augusta/Hamburg in Lake Greenwood at low water level. *Collection of Jim Scott.*

- **Edgefield**: Edgefield is an early historic village. The road into town, Buncombe Road, is full of beautiful antebellum and late 1800s mansions. Enter town slowly to enjoy the architecture. On the town square, find Dixie Highway Hotel. Three roads leave the square to Augusta/Hamburg. The eastern one is current U.S. 25 to the Pine House. The middle one is Old Stage Road, which is still partly a dirt passage where some ruts can also be found. Some are near the Horn Creek Church. The western road is Sweetwater Road. Also, find Old Edgefield Road in Edgefield County and Old Edgefield Road in North Augusta.
- **Hamburg/North Augusta**: Take Old Edgefield Road to the ghost town of Hamburg through North Augusta. The early twentieth-century bridges here are beautiful, one named Abandoned (so called on bridgehunters.com) and the Jefferson Davis Memorial Bridge. Look for the old port of Hamburg. Take

Although Edgefield, South Carolina, had had a hotel on the square since 1812, fires ravaged the wooden buildings in the late 1800s, leaving the town square without a hotel. Dixie Highway Hotel was built in 1920 on the town square as the Dixie Highway hype pushed the town forward. This village is still much as it was in 1920.

This South Carolina State Historical Marker is near the site of the port of Hamburg, which was used to divert products from Augusta into South Carolina. Built in 1827, it thrived only until the late 1800s and was swallowed by North Augusta.

Sand Pit Road to East Railroad Avenue to go to the railroad bridge still spanning the Savannah River. It is an interesting one. Please notice the small park between the two automobile bridges. It might be destroyed when the Augusta walking park across the Jefferson Davis Memorial Bridge is complete. To see the drawbridge side of the train trestle, travel into Georgia across the Memorial Bridge.

THE CONCRETE: EXTANT SITES

There are at least twelve extant portions of concrete along U.S. 25 in the western part of the Carolinas that closely define the path of the original concrete road. Much of the current U.S. 25 follows a straighter path, cutting off sections of the old highway and thus allowing for the preservation of the original concrete within these sections. Many other of these cut-off curves of the concrete highway are still used but have been paved over with modern asphalt.

- **Fletcher**: The concrete road section that has been found in North Carolina is just off Old Hendersonville Road on the property of Carolina Concrete Systems. This company owns a large business that was originally crossed in the eastern part of its land by U.S. 25. On examination, a portion of the concrete road was over a marshy area, maybe a spring, and was therefore unstable. A later road bypassed at the top of a rise and returned to the original road circling the wet section. The redirection of the road left the section across the marsh for the concrete company, where road barriers blocked construction vehicles from crossing and possibly miring up in mud.

- **Old Augusta Road at North Saluda Reservoir, North and South**: There are two sections running into the reservoir; the north length is approximately 685 feet to the water's edge, and the south is approximately 1,456 feet. It was constructed in 1927–28.

  Old Augusta Road was the original path coming down the Blue Ridge Mountains from North Carolina through the Saluda Gap; it was often called Saluda Turnpike between Glassy and Hogback Mountains. This part of the road was most torturous for travelers and traders and for construction. It enters South Carolina below the village of Tuxedo, North Carolina.

  The Greenville Water System brought the North Saluda Reservoir online in 1961, encompassing nineteen thousand acres of mountainous terrain, homesites, graveyards and the town of Merrittsville. Since U.S. 25 ran through that Upstate village, the road was rerouted around the lake and the reservoir fenced. The watershed is described in the *Greenville Journal* as a completely undeveloped area without recreation or other human activity.[191]

  Consisting of steep grades and numerous switchbacks, Old Augusta Road winds through Upstate hardwood forests, passing Poinsett's summer homesite and the North Saluda River, but there is limited access, noted by signage requiring you to stay in your vehicle because of the North Saluda Reservoir supplying the Greenville area with clean drinking water.

Coincidentally, concrete of the original highway in North Carolina still lies on the property of a concrete business near Fletcher.

Currently, the original road has been paved over with blacktop, and the North Saluda Reservoir has covered the town of Merrittsville. Here, north of the reservoir lake, the concrete road is evident on current aerials, but access to the area is fenced to protect the watershed. South of the reservoir, the old concrete highway surfaces from Merrittsville, and this can be seen again

Off Old U.S. 25 in northern Greenville County, South Carolina, concrete from the old road laid in 1928 exits from the base of the dam of the North Saluda Reservoir off Callahan Mountain Road.

on current aerials exiting below the dam into Callahan Mountain Road and connecting back into Old Augusta Road. Callahan Mountain Road still has extant concrete below the dam, and it can be seen through the fence. Follow Callahan Mountain Road east to see Poinsett Bridge (1820) and log farming structures.

- **Bridge over the North Saluda River**: This small 123-foot bridge dated 1928 is on Callahan Mountain Road as it nears Old Augusta Road after leaving the dam. This bridge leads over the North Saluda where it is allowed to run from the reservoir. The corner of the railing is broken near the date where something damaged the concrete. The North Saluda at this site is similar to a large creek and flows only slightly downhill.
- **Frontage Road**: This particular section of the concrete highway is along the current U.S. 25 at the overpass for scenic Highway 11, which crosses the Upstate at the base of the mountains from Walhalla across beautiful Lake Keowee to Cowpens National Battlefield and Gaffney. It is approximately

136

Dated 1928, this bridge on Callahan Mountain Road was part of the original U.S. 25 leading north to Merrittsville, which is now under the North Saluda Reservoir, the city of Greenville's water supply.

946 feet long and was constructed in 1927. Historic Goodwin House Inn is perched to the west of the overpass and overlooks the roads and a new interchange. Most of the area is surrounded by hardwood forests in transition from higher-altitude evergreens such as hemlocks. A few of those are evident at the Goodwin House site, which is an early 1800s inn owned by the Greenville County Recreation Department and is being restored for possible use as a welcome center.

Frontage Road is currently used for parking and access to a construction business and a home. This section of the old concrete highway is just west of the current U.S. 25. Old Settlement Road is across U.S. 25, and it leads through a farming bottom to Highway 11 west of the Goodwin House.

- **Moki Road**: Moki Road was a curve in old Dixie Highway that was cut off after the construction of the current U.S. 25. It was constructed in 1927 and is approximately 1,653 feet long. It

This farmhouse that once belonged to Dan Hunt is on a cutoff of U.S. 25, Moki Road, which is still concrete. Dan and his wife ran a wayside attraction here in the 1940s–70s. All handmade rides enticed children and parents to stop. For the story, see chapter 11.

still services a historic home that once offered travelers fair-like entertainment even into the 1960s with a Ferris wheel and pony rides. The topography of this section of the old concrete road shows a valley terrain with industrial businesses nearby. Mush Creek Road turns off to the east just north of a low concrete bridge over the North Enoree River, which at this point is a small creek. The historic homesite with some acreage and outbuildings is the first eastern view. An asphalt plant is also east of the south intersection with U.S. 25. The view from Moki Road to the west is of U.S. 25 and a wood yard business.

- **Old Buncombe Road Concrete Bridge**: This thirty-six-foot bridge south of Travelers Rest was constructed in 1910 prior to U.S. Highway 25 but is included here because in its beginning, roads were constructed in the towns first and spread out like spokes. A train, the Swamp Rabbit, ran from Travelers Rest north into the mountains, and turn-of-the-twentieth-century Greenvillians would travel to the Spring Park Inn there, picnic and ride the train for a ways to the north and back. This probably encouraged the paving of Buncombe Road to Travelers Rest at an early date.

North of the city of Greenville, the road to North Carolina is called the Old Buncombe Road, as it ran toward Buncombe County, North Carolina. Being the old trader's wagon road to and from the mountains, this road was important to Upstate commerce. Just south of downtown Travelers Rest after the

Below Travelers Rest, South Carolina, on Old Buncombe Road, an early bridge is extant. Dated 1910, this is the original road from Greenville to the railroad, the Swamp Rabbit, for rides into the mountains.

intersection with Watson Road, Old Buncombe Road passes into a pastoral setting, crossing a creek that feeds the headwaters of the Reedy River. Although the road itself has been paved over, the concrete bridge is extant and dated 1910. The view west is of homesites surrounded by pastureland, with the creek and banks covered by lush vegetation in the warm months. Other asphalted sections of Old Buncombe are still along the current U.S. 25.

From this bridge into and through Greenville to Donaldson Center, the old concrete highway has been paved over with asphalt. There are numerous mill villages and historic buildings as you pass through Greenville, as well as the historic Reedy River Falls and the new Liberty Bridge. In downtown Greenville, Augusta Street forks off South Main Street, passing through historic housing developments from the 1800s. South of town, it turns into Augusta Road. Follow Augusta Road straight over I-85. You can follow Old Augusta Road as a quick loop off the road to the east.

- **Donaldson Center and SCTAC (South Carolina Technology and Aviation Center)**: This area on Perimeter Road at Augusta Arbor Way was constructed in 1929 and is approximately ninety-three feet long.

  This area south of Greenville was rural, with cotton farms covering the rolling hills and supplying the textile mills with their products. It was much more conducive to growth of cotton, but plantations were dwindling in size after the turn of the twentieth century. Basically, the Augusta Road straightened as it reached the ridge on the old Indian path dividing the watersheds of the Saluda River to the west and the Reedy River to the east. It passed through small crossroads and by inns along the way.

  Affecting U.S. 25 was the construction of the Greenville Army Air Base south of the city. This base was renamed in 1951 for Greenville native and World War I ace pilot John Owen Donaldson. In 1942, Augusta Road was rerouted off the base's property.[192] This left an intact portion of the old concrete on a section of the base at Perimeter Road and Augusta Arbor Way. This small section of concrete is near aircraft hangars on property owned by the City of Greenville and Greenville County. The concrete road runs from Perimeter Road into the fenced area next to the hangars.

  From that concrete, the paved-over Old Augusta Road extends south toward Moonville. Recently, that section of Old Augusta was renamed Augusta Arbor Way and was repaved with asphalt. A short part of it is industrial near Perimeter Road, but then it is wooded on both sides until it comes to Antioch Church Road.

- **Old Augusta Road/Augusta Arbor Way**: This section, south of Antioch Church Road in Moonville, is approximately 1,042 feet and was constructed in 1929. South of Augusta Arbor Way, where it crosses Antioch Church Road, the concrete road reappears as Old Augusta Road. It is another section cut off by road construction (Interstate I-85). Here Old Augusta Road continues to service several businesses connected to Donaldson Center and SCTAC and ends in a cul-de-sac that overlooks the interstate through a fence.

- **Old Augusta Road**: On the south side of I-185, behind the McDonald's and Clock restaurants, a 711-foot stretch of Old Augusta Road continues to the old center of Moonville where a

Above: South of Greenville, concrete from the original U.S. 25 can be found on Donaldson Center. The Augusta Road here was moved in 1942 when Greenville Army Air Base was built, but concrete can be found that ran across the base in front of these hangars.

Left: U.S. 25 from Donaldson Center (now SCTAC) ran straight into the small village of Moonville. The concrete was cut off by new road construction in 1942. This section is at Augusta Arbor Way and Antioch Church Road north of I-185.

traffic light has been placed. When Augusta Road was rerouted for the construction of the air base in 1942, the new road came into Moonville on the western side of a store building, Vaughn's Store. The concrete road section was not removed since there were two homes along it; this put the store in a *V* of the old concrete road and the new asphalt one. That store and the houses are no longer extant. Now, two other buildings face the old concrete section. McDonald's and the Clock restaurant were built in that *V*. The Old Augusta Road separates the restaurants from a small industry and a fire station. Having been a rural area along the concrete road prior to 1942, Moonville is now a small village that became a service area to the air base and

Concrete in the center of Moonville still exists as Old Augusta Road angling from the stoplight north on the east side of McDonald's and the Clock restaurants.

has grown over the years with grocery stores and restaurants accommodating the businesses at SCTAC and several other industrial parks along the I-185 toll road.

From Moonville the Old Augusta Road continued approximately along the wagon road to the terminus of Greenville County and briefly into Laurens County before traveling into the Greenwood County towns of Ware Shoals, Hodges and Greenwood. It continued toward Edgefield, where the next extant section of the old road's concrete can be found. Be sure to drive through downtown Ware Shoals with its historic public buildings, and through Hodges, with the beautiful Victorian churches and houses. Take Dixie Drive, the old Dixie Highway, to see the fire tower. If you have time, take a detour to Cokesbury, an early 1800s college, now owned by Greenwood Historical Society. U.S. Highway 25 went through downtown Greenwood, which has a significant mill and train history, and there is a train museum on Main Street. Note also the U.S. 25 Drive-In Movie Theater south of town.

In the Riegel Cotton Mill town of Ware Shoals, the downtown has much old concrete. This inn was built circa 1920 and is now a senior citizens' home. Many structures here were built in the 1920s and 1930s along the Dixie Highway. Check out the Ware Shoals High School and the Field House. The Field House is especially striking but is off the main drag.

Greenwood's Main Street is just off the old Augusta Road. Follow the "old" named streets through town, although they have been paved with asphalt. This South Carolina town came along with the railroads in the 1850s and is famous for its numerous tracks and railroad museum. South of town is an old drive-in theater still in use.

- **Stevens/Turkey Creek Bridge and Road, North and South**: On U.S. 25 in northern Edgefield County, the northern section is approximately 126 feet and the southern section is approximately 2,179 feet. It was constructed in 1929. This extant section of U.S. Highway 25 is protected because of the new bridges over Stevens and Turkey Creeks. Concrete is evident in two portions—one toward Greenwood and the other toward Edgefield from the creek. Access is best from the Edgefield end, where the concrete veers off to the east in a long lane to the old concrete bridge and the creek. The depression for the wagon trail is still visible to the east, and the bridge itself is easily accessible here. This road runs 1,200 feet to an extant section of the original bridge with the center section missing, but visible over the creek is the continuance of the bridge and road up a gradual incline returning to U.S. 25. To the east of the

This page: Stevens and Turkey Creek Bridges. There are about four or maybe five bridges at this site. Evidence of these is extant in a very rural area of Edgefield County, South Carolina. The original U.S. 25 bridge and concrete road are best seen from the southern end.

remaining old U.S. 25 concrete bridge are round black pylons in a unique position, possibly indicating a covered or iron bridge. The current U.S. 25/Augusta Road bridge over Stevens/Turkey Creek far to the west can be seen from the abandoned concrete road. Round pylons and massive concrete supports immediately to the west of that provide evidence of another bridge in the not so distant past. The concrete section toward Greenwood is readily seen on current aerials.

This rural area was forested until the fall of 2019, when the woods on both sides of U.S. 25 and the concrete road were clear cut, opening the view of all four bridges. Because SCDOT was not formed until 1917, when a five-member highway commission was appointed,[193] no records for the early iron or wooden covered bridges have been found.

Following U.S. 25 on to North Augusta, you will pass through historic Edgefield, and the Dixie Highway Hotel is still on the square. The hotel is now called Plantation House. At Trenton, go slowly as you turn toward Augusta and note the Pine House and the stone road marker in the yard there. In Augusta is the old ghost town of Hamburg.

- **Abandoned Concrete Bridge**: This abandoned concrete bridge near the Savannah River now on Fifth Street in North Augusta served as overflow and is a T-beam construction completed in 1931 for U.S. 25. It is 1,200.8 feet in length. It was bypassed in about 1971 by a new bridge for U.S. 1. Notice the wing walls used in its construction. For details on the bridge, see bridgehunters.com.

Along the Savannah River at the site of historic Hamburg, South Carolina, which has been absorbed by North Augusta, Sand Pit Road snakes under the Abandoned Concrete Bridge cut off by a new road, U.S. 78. This U.S. 25 bridge is now covered with vines and trees growing along the entrances and at the bases of the pillars along Sand Pit Road, blocking most of the views on either side of the upper roadway. The upper parts of the bridge can be accessed and viewed from Fifth Avenue, but the bridge ends under the newer U.S. 78 bridge. A small park is at the west end of the bridge but now across Fifth Avenue. The park does not appear to be in use. There are a few flowering crepe myrtles still extant among the cracked concrete sections.

Above: In North Augusta, at the old site of the port of Hamburg, is this beautiful abandoned bridge. Drive under on Sand Pit Road, which reminds one of the issues early motorists faced. Be careful.

Left: This bridge was abandoned when newer bridges were built to the south. A very lengthy section is now covered in vegetation but is worth investigation.

This worn concrete is the only evidence that the park may have been built at the time of the bridges.

From Sand Pit Road to the left turning away from the bridge is a lightly traveled side road, East Railroad Avenue, which leads to the heart of old Hamburg. Abandoned concrete buildings on the left are covered in vegetation in the warm months and tree trunks during the cold periods, and a fenced business is to the right. At the end of this lane coming into a clearing, a dirt vehicle path turns left toward the river, and several camping sites can be seen behind a white concrete block building. The old railroad bridge runs alongside this dirt road as it rises to move over the Savannah River.

- **Jefferson Davis Memorial Bridge**: The Jefferson Davis Memorial Bridge on Fifth Street over the Savannah River connects North Augusta, South Carolina, to Augusta, Georgia, at the historic site of old Hamburg, South Carolina, an early commercial port. It is 1,201.8 feet long. This bridge over the Savannah River was Old U.S. 25's connection to Georgia from South Carolina. It is a concrete bridge with bronze balusters and memorial plaques. Plaques on both ends of the Jefferson Davis Bridge state that it was completed in 1931. The abandoned concrete bridge, the abandoned park and the Jefferson Davis Memorial Bridge are less than twenty-five yards apart.

This memorial bridge is an *X* or cross frame steel stringer bridge, and it is listed as eligible for the National Register of Historic Places.[194] For a detailed description of the Jefferson Davis Memorial Bridge across the Savannah connecting South Carolina and Georgia, see bridgehunters.com.

Inspected in December 2017, the Jefferson Davis Memorial Bridge was found to be generally in poor condition, but it contributes to the Historic District across the Savannah River in Augusta. As noted here, with the age of this bridge, deep maintenance needs to be done for it to continue to carry automobile traffic. Therefore, the plan at this time is to make it into a walking park.

This page: The Jefferson Davis Memorial Bridge over the Savannah River is about one hundred or so feet from the abandoned bridge and a small concrete park between the two. This bridge is currently being turned into a walking bridge connected to a park on the Augusta side of the river.

IMPORTANCE OF THE AUGUSTA-BUNCOMBE ROAD

As road travelers today, we will never know this roadway as those who stepped every inch of the trail following the tracks of thousands of feet before them; those who walked the entire path or just sections of it; or those who plied it on horseback, open carriage or farm wagon with their animals. Here at the end of our travels together, Jim and I hope that your journey with us through this history of an ancient road has provided insight into its importance to the growth of the backcountry in the Carolinas. It connects us, for we are all descendants of our history.

We must understand that, although the names are different and progress in technology and social systems has grown, Americans are still a people with the same needs, drives and foibles that our ancestors passed down to us. Trade and travel answered sundry of those issues and became a common drive across our culture. May the road trip forever broaden our perspectives and provide insights and understanding and compassion along the way.

> *I took to the open road in search of places where change did not mean ruin and where time and men and deeds connected.*
> —*William Least Heat-Moon,* Blue Highways[195]

Chapter 11

STORIES OF THE ROAD

Stories, Recollections and Sagas

DAN'S PLACE

Dan's Place Just Grew Up Out Back
By Lynne Lucus
Summarized from the *Greenville News*, March 1, 1981, with additions from
the author

"Dan Hunt took the cigarette he had just lit, pressed it between his poodle's
lips, and watched his pet drive the race car around the track." Poodle Woodle
liked the race cars, but his favorite was the Ferris wheel that his master, Dan,
had built. Wearing sun glasses as the wheel turned, the white curly haired
dog seemed to enjoy just watching the medley of rides, games, animals, and
birds set before him.

The poodle was only one of hundreds of the menagerie of creatures on
the 40-acre home place/amusement park, Dan and his wife, Tweedy, ran
for over 20 years along US 25 north of Traveler's Rest, SC. There were
parakeets by the hundreds, carp by the same numbers in the 3-acre fishing
pond, and worms and minnows to go along. White doves and rabbits and
ponies were all being raised. Some of the ponies provided rides for the
children who came by to enjoy the park too.

The entire park was built by Dan from scrap metal and old car parts,
including old car transmissions for the automated rides. There were rides

of all descriptions—airplanes, cars, trains, boats to name a few. His Ferris wheel was the best, but the kids favored the ponies.

Later he added a putt-putt and batting cage.

Greg Thompson said on Facebook, "I remember that very well. He made all of that stuff—no seatbelt, no helmet, just fun. He also had a homemade batting cage. Never knew which way or how fast it would launch that ball—better be ready to move!"

Dan and Tweedy loved running the park. Tweedy said she and Dan just enjoyed the people and loved the kids coming by to see them and their animals.

(The remnants of the Hunt home can be found on Moki Road north of Travelers Rest, South Carolina.)

COUSIN TEMPIE

Cousin Tempie McKittrick
By Caroline S. Coleman
Edited by J.A. Scott III, 2020

Mrs. Temperance Scott McKittrick, better known as Cousin Tempie, lived on the Augusta Road about 20 miles south of Greenville, SC. For over two centuries the traditions of "open house" have been associated with this home, the historic Chandler Place (McKittrick house) which has come down to Cousin Tempie from generations of her family. Having company is my hobby, declares this youthful woman of seventy-two years.

Cousin Tempie lived alone for many years. Entertaining visitors meant cooking meals, milking the cow, drawing water from a well in the yard all with one pair of hands, yet last year 3,000 guests registered in Cousin Tempie's little black guest book—most of whom stayed for at least one meal.

Friends drop in to call and are urged to spend the day—or the week. Summer visitors arrive to spend a month, and the unexpected guest arriving at Cousin Tempie's in time for a mid-day dinner, will probably find the long table set for a dozen persons with a side table ready to accommodate the overflow. Her table can be extended to seat eighteen; a tight squeeze in a farm-house dining room but nothing fazes cousin Tempie.

Widowed early in life, and with a helpless invalid son to care for, Cousin Tempie bravely shouldered her burdens and made her home a place where the world might find cheer instead of gloom. Fred, the shut-in son, was internationally known before his death a few years ago at the age of forty-five. His wheel chair was always the center of a merry group of friends who came from many states to talk with the interesting invalid. Often his jolly laugh could be heard far down the Dixie Highway, as he called out a greeting to a passing motorist.

Fred McKittrick acquired pen pals throughout the continent and in the British Isles. Cousin Tempie answered his letters, invited these distant friends to come, and many did make long journeys to visit this home where both mother and son were ready with an eager welcome. Gene Stratton Porter, before her death, was one of these friends who kept in touch with this home, and sent copies of her books to Fred. [Geneva Stratton Porter was a novelist, nature photographer and naturalist whose books were often turned into movies during the early 1900s. The Gene Stratton-Porter Historic Site in Rome City, Indiana, near Fort Wayne, is run by the Indiana State Museum.]

The work of letter-writing was begun for Fred, but Cousin Tempie still keeps it up as another hobby. [Fred Stennis McKittrick passed away in 1936, and nearly two thousand persons attended his funeral at Lickville Presbyterian Church on the Augusta Road. He had been a deacon and treasurer of the church.] She will tell you about the dozens of shut-ins to whom she writes regularly bringing joy into dull lives; about the friends in Ireland who came across the sea to visit this letter-writer in her country home and with an abundance of welcome.

Cousin Tempie still has in her possession the original grant to her plantation signed by King George III. The grant was made to her Great Great Grandfather William Davenport who came to South Carolina down the Great Wagon road from New Haven, Connecticut.

William Davenport was the owner of much property at the time of his death. The home place was given to his daughter Temperance who married Allen Chandler, and the plantation became known as the Chandler Place. For many years the Chandler Place was the center of gracious hospitality. Hog drovers, horse drovers, turkey drovers and peddlers—all the picturesque array of travelers in a picturesque day, came down the road to stop at the Chandler Place for food and lodging. When the beds were full others slept on the floor. The present house contains enough bedrooms so that today's guests do not have to sleep on the floor, but even yet the rooms are often full to overflowing.

The annual custom of the house is a "harvest supper." On a certain "moonlit night in the full moon in October" Cousin Tempie's board is spread with home-grown viands, only. These are prepared according to recipes popular in the long ago, nothing of modern dab of this and that, are permitted on the table on this occasion. The guests are a group of the county pioneers. Elderly gentlemen from Greenville, and all of whom have attained much success in life, sometimes referred to as "city Fathers." But down on the farm they are still "the Boys." At Cousin Tempie's they gather around the long table and just forget for a while, heart trouble, arthritis, gout, and other health issues and give themselves one fling at good eating.

The meal over the "boys" enjoy an hour or two in telling the old stories and living again the days of youth, when life was not such a rush. No— cousin Tempie did not know these "Boys" at youth. It is through their visits to Fred that she met them, and the Harvest Supper grew out of her desire to offer hospitality to all comers.

When Cousin Tempie's daughter, Cousin Mary Knight, and her family moved in to stay with her in later years, it was stipulated that no changes be made in the custom of entertaining. In fact, there are now more guests than before.

Modern conveniences installed in her later years made housekeeping easy, but Cousin Tempie never quailed at drawing water, or cooking meals on an old wood stove. She could do all and still entertain 3,000 guests a year. Hospitality is one of the greatest of all virtues.

[Cousin Tempie's home still rests near the Augusta Road, where the dirt road passed Fred's porch within probably fifty feet.]

COUSIN DAVE

Cousin Dave Ridgeway
William David Ridgeway Jr. (January 25, 1891–October 29, 1965)
Laura Mae Raines Ridgeway (April 11, 1891–June 14, 1969)
By Jim Scott

W.D. Ridgeway was the oldest child of William David (Dock) Ridgeway Sr. and Elizabeth Sims. He was born in Fork Shoals in southern Greenville County, South Carolina. His mother and father died young and left Dave to take care of seven brothers and sisters. He kept the family together, and all married off, and Dave had a lot of nieces and nephews. Later in life, Dave became known far and wide as "Unca Dave."

Early in life, Dave built a cotton gin and general store at the Lebanon Church community and became successful as a farmer and businessman early on. He was also a member of nearby Daventon Baptist Church and became a member of Ornan Lodge #69 AFM at Fork Shoals, South Carolina, and later a member of Hejaz Shrine Temple, AAONMS, in Greenville, South Carolina.

Dave was known also as a philanthropist, constantly doing good work for the community that he lived in and helping others in need on almost all occasions. As secretary of Ornan Lodge, I studied the old minutes in writing the lodge history up to 1999 and found Dave's name many times in the minutes as having made many generous contributions to charitable causes over the years in Fork Shoals and surrounding communities. He became known in the Upstate as a generous philanthropist.

I know that in the deep days of the Great Depression a large dam was being constructed on Saluda River called Buzzard's Roost Dam. Dave found out about several bridges that were going to be moved during the flooding of this lake. Dave negotiated to get these bridges given to Greenville County and took his huge cotton trucks down into Greenwood and Laurens County and hauled the bridges back at no charge to the Lebanon Church community and opened two roads in and out of that community, saving a lot of travel miles to the residents. One of these roads was later named W.D. Ridgeway Road after Dave. The other road is now called Hillside Church Road.

Progress was finally coming to southern Greenville County by the 1930s. Duke Power Company built a power line from Piedmont to McCullough's. They also built one from Anderson County to Tumbling Shoals Dam on the Reedy River, coming straight through Princeton, a small community in Laurens County just south and bordering the Greenville County line on the Dixie Highway, also known as the Augusta Road.

This gave an opportunity for Dave. The old gin was powered by either a steam or internal combustion engine. Modern-day gins ran on electric power and are much more efficient. Dave negotiated a deal with Duke Power to furnish him power for his gin at a special rate if he would move to Princeton. Duke Power accepted, as more progress was coming to the county. Dave had a lot of nieces and nephews and cousins who were coming of work age. He also negotiated a deal with Fred McCullough to rent about one thousand acres of prime farmland just north of Princeton on the headwaters of Horse Creek. On this land he raised cotton, corn, wheat and oats and had a large pasture for his many beef cows. He moved his sawmill to Princeton and started cutting and sawing timber. He got his cousins the Sims boys and nephews the Woods boys and their father, who had been large sharecroppers for the late Judge Joe McCullough for previous years, to saw and build the gin. He needed a general store, so he got his nephews the Babb boys from Gray Court to move to Princeton and run the store he built for them. He needed trucks to haul merchandise and cotton and cattle, so he bought many big trucks for his operation. The Babbs operated the trucking business too. Later, Dave built a modern laundry and dry cleaners in Princeton.

Princeton was beginning to progress very well since the failure of the railroad that was to come through Princeton in the 1880s. The railroad was a line between Augusta, Georgia, Greenville, South Carolina, and Knoxville, Tennessee. Much of the old railroad bed can still be seen along areas of Augusta Road.

About the same time as Dave was building in Princeton along the Augusta Road, a Mr. Sharp was also building. He built a store and filling station and restaurant and also a tourist court right in the middle of Princeton. Mr. Sharp had a man, Mr. Jones, who was a rock mason from Abbeville living on his farm. Mr. Sharp built all of his buildings from rocks hauled from the fields around the area. Mr. Ike Jones became famous for his many rock houses and other structures like the Ware Shoals Field House and Stadium and others all the way to Greenville and in the city of Greenville. Mr. Jones worked until he was in his nineties, but in his late years, he had some young men helping him.

Cousin Dave loved baseball! He always had a team and a stadium at Lebanon. After coming to Princeton, he built a ball diamond right beside his sawmill. They played other teams in the area and finally got into the Textile League and competed successfully with the numerous mill teams in the area. I know of at least three who got into the pros and one into the Major League. At night, he would get a carload of boys and go to Greenville to watch the Spinners play and would pay for admission and hot dogs for all.

When I was a young boy, sometimes we would be at the store and Cousin Dave would come in and say his greeting of "Yesiree, I'm gonna set you boys up, get yourself a Coke and a pack of crackers." Boy, we loved that man. He would give us balls and bats for pasture baseball. He was our champ.

Bad Luck

Besides being a ginner and farmer, Cousin Dave was also a cotton factor, in that he would advance local farmers seed, fertilizer and other necessary items to put in a cotton crop. When the crop was ginned, he would buy the cotton and take out his advances with no interest. This was a common practice with most all ginners at the time. In 1957, Greenville County experienced one of the worst droughts in many years. Farmers including Cousin Dave produced hardly any cotton. This unfortunate incident put Dave in a bad financial condition. He still owed a lot of money on his fertilizer bill, and they were pressing him hard for the balance. After they got all of what little cotton there was ginned and hauled, he had his men put high sideboards on several of his cotton trucks. They got sawmill slabs and built huge corrals in the big McCullough pasture and caught the cattle that he had. I remember seeing load after load come out of that pasture, as it was very close to where we lived. He got enough money for the cows to pay the balance of the fertilizer bill and was able to stay in business.

Murder

This incident probably occurred in the '30s. There was an old man who was very mean who lived in the Flat Rock community, which is between Princeton and Lebanon Church community. I will not divulge the man's name for his family's sake; they still live nearby and are fine people. This man actually tried to break into my mother's family home in the Flat Rock community before the murder incident. The old man was drunk and sleeping in my grandfather's barn one Sunday afternoon. My grandfather was away taking care of his terminally ill father a few miles down the road. My mother and her sisters were alone at the house, and the old man woke up in the barn and knew there were several young ladies in the house and came and started knocking on the door. These girls were absolutely horrified, so my mother, the oldest, took it upon herself to get her daddy's shotgun and point to the door and told the intruder to let go of the doorknob and walk off the porch or she would shoot through the door. She said she saw the doorknob start moving slowly counterclockwise and heard him walk off the back porch. The girls huddled together and said a prayer to the Almighty for their deliverance from this dangerous individual.

We are told that this man had a nice and beautiful wife who was a schoolteacher. The man got drunk and got mad at his wife and picked her up and sat her on the hot stove and severely burned her. He was inspired by the ole devil himself. And there are all kinds of terrible tales about this mean man.

As I mentioned earlier, Mr. Sharp had a store and tourist camp at Princeton. A lot of traveling salesmen would stop and overnight at this place. One such salesman was there one night. The store was actually a beer hall at night, and the salesman was enjoying some beer and noticed a card game at a nearby table. He asked if he could join, and he was accepted into the game, but the old mean man was also in the game. It didn't take long for the players to see that the salesman had a lot of money on him, and the old mean man got to thinking evil thoughts. The salesman had rented a room at Mr. Sharp's tourist cabin, but the old mean man convinced him to stay the night at his house and that his wife was a wonderful cook and would feed him well. So, the salesman and the mean man left together in the salesman's car. They went down Latimer's Mill Road toward Flat Rock community, and in a sharp curve near Horse Creek, the old mean man shot the salesman and killed him and robbed him and left and walked to his house.

Early the next morning, Cousin Dave was going to the bank at Fountain Inn. Driving down Latimer's Mill Road, he noticed a car in the ditch with someone in the car. Upon a strict search, he found the salesman to be dead, and someone had stuck a cigarette in the bullet hole to stop the bleeding and look like the accident had killed the salesman. Cousin Dave called the sheriff. After the sheriff got there, he found out the salesman had been at the beer hall the previous evening and inquired and learned that the salesman left with the mean man and that was the last time anyone saw either of them.

The sheriff arrested the mean man, and he was convicted, and after the sentence was pronounced, the mean man stated that when he got out of prison he was coming straight to Princeton and kill Dave Ridgeway, whose testimony had played an important part in his conviction.

The mean man was sent to Columbia to prison. After serving his sentence, the prison would give parolees a new suit and some amount of cash money to get home. He got on a bus to come home, and the bus stopped for a rest stop somewhere between Columbia and Greenville and the old mean man got off the bus and stepped into the street and was run over and killed by a motorist. Stranger things have happened!

JOE MCCULLOUGH COMES TO THE ROAD

By Jim Scott

The McCullough Family Part I

The Joe McCullough homeplace, built in 1812, is the oldest brick structure in Greenville County, South Carolina, and is called Cedarhurst by the family, although locals know it as the McCullough House.

The McCullough family had lived in Scotland for many years. Sometime in the seventeenth century, they moved to Ireland. They lived in a small village in County Antrim called Rasharkin, which is very close to Port Rush and not too far from Belfast. They were neighbors to the Scotts, Reids, Buchanans and Craigs.

The McCulloughs were devout Methodists and were farmers in Ireland, but in the late eighteenth century, farmers were not doing well with their crops. There were several brothers who wanted to immigrate to America, and three of them left Ireland sometime in the 1780s. One of them was David, who settled in Laurens County, South Carolina, near Young's Community on the Enoree River. David had a store in Young's Community.

One night on his way home, he was attacked by a highwayman and robbed and murdered. His oldest brother, William, had to come to America to settle David's estate in the early 1790s.

You know probate courts don't get in a hurry, and William was in Laurens for several years and met a lady, Miss Ross, who he married, and they had a son, David. Well, when the estate of his brother David was finally settled, William by law had to return to Ireland to get the proper credentials to come back to America. Hoping this would be only a matter of months, William left his wife and son in Laurens County.

As it turned out, when William got back to Ireland, the country was in rebellion, as it has been many times, and he could not get the necessary credentials to return to America until the rebellion was over, which was about five years we are told.

William finally got the necessary credentials, and he set out for America. This time he brought his youngest brother Joe. Well, when William and Joe finally reached Laurens County, South Carolina, they were in for a surprise. William's wife, thinking that William was dead, had remarried to a Mr. Simpson. Well, the matter was brought before a justice of the peace, who understood the situation, and he did not charge the wife with bigamy and gave her a choice of which husband she wanted to keep. She chose the latter, Mr. Simpson.

There William and Joe were in Laurens County; what should they do? Someone suggested to them that the soil in southern Greenville County was the absolute best for producing cotton in the entire state of South Carolina, so William and Joe set out for southern Greenville County.

They each bought land and started growing cotton, the principal crop of the South, and did very well. They accumulated a lot of land, William over 1,200 acres and Joe considerably more than his brother. Joe's land was on the headwaters of Horse Creek on the famous Augusta Road that runs from Buncombe County, North Carolina, to Augusta, Georgia. All of the cotton produced in the Upstate had to be transported down this famous road to Hamburg, South Carolina, and loaded on barges and floated to Savannah, Georgia, to be shipped to Europe. From Joe's plantation to Hamburg was approximately ninety miles. Hauling cotton on a wagon was slow, and a good day's travel was only twenty-five miles, so a trip from McCullough's to Hamburg was about a three-and-a-half-day trip. Only about two or three bales of cotton could be carried on a large wagon. A bale was five hundred pounds of lint.

I have a letter that Joe wrote to his nephew in Ireland, and he said that he made over five hundred bales of cotton the previous crop year. That is a lot of trips to Hamburg on an old dirt road ninety miles long. You had to have places to stay overnight to rest and accommodations for livestock. The cotton was picked and ginned in the fall, so most of the hauling was done in the late fall and winter, and conditions were generally wet in South Carolina during these months.

Understanding these conditions and need for infrastructure, Joe built a big house with a separate kitchen building in back. This kitchen building had an upstairs with rooms for lodging. Also, Joe constructed pens for livestock and had ample feed on hand for the livestock. This was a profitable business for Joe. Joe also had a store and a cotton gin to gin his cotton and his neighbors' crop too.

Down the Augusta Road about twenty-seven miles was another such stop built by William Smith and called Stony Point. It was in Abbeville County about one day from McCullough's. Most likely, Joe would stay overnight at Stony Point on his travels to Hamburg/Augusta. The McCulloughs and Smiths became close friends, and some of Joe's children married Smith children and the family became closely connected. These families were like all wealthy of the time, as the upcoming story tells, and their wealth was built on the backs of their enslaved workers.

The McCullough Family of Greenville County, Part II

Well, Joe McCullough was doing quite well in America and was anxious about getting more of his family from Ireland to come here. He got James McCullough and James Reid, both nephews of Joe, and as far as I know neither of them married but are buried in the McCullough Cemetery behind the old mansion. James was a son of Robert McCullough, who stayed in Ireland. James had a sister Sarah who married John Scott; they came here in 1847 and lived near the McCullough place. John and Sarah were my second great-grandparents.

Joe in his pleasure loved horse racing and built a horse racetrack on his property. People from all over the state would bring horses to these races. It was a big event in Greenville County in the early days.

Tricks in the Trade: An Ole Tale about Joe McCullough

This tale is from the family history that Sue Scott compiled and published in 1961. We are greatly indebted to Sue for her search for the Scott relatives and for her humorous anecdotes that bring mere statistics to life.

Sue had no interest in dates (there are none on her tombstone), so...

It was in late fall of the year 1851 in the Piedmont section of the deep sunny South, and the air spoke of the sting of approaching winter. Six or seven farmers were seated on broken chairs, handmade benches, cow feed boxes and nail kegs around an open fire in the rear end of a country store.

"I wonder how Widow Carson's sale came out," said Dick Hathaway as he spat a squirt of tobacco juice across the wide rock hearth, which was littered with walnut and hickory nut hulls, bits of paper and whittlings from sticks on which each loafer tested the sharpness of the blade of his big hunting knife.

"I dunno," said Tom Donald as he moved his nail keg seat and placed it on the tail of a mongrel hound that was sprawled on the rough splintered floor.

"I heered old man Joe bought lots of the stuff, but I know he didn't pay much fer it. You know ole Joe—as the old saying goes, 'he'd skin a flea fer its hide and taller,'" responded Alex Wakefield.

"Old Joe," as he was referred to when out of earshot, and "Uncle Joe," as he was addressed when in earshot, was Joe McCullough, a product of "County Antrim in the auld countree." When a young man, he had immigrated to America, and by the ripe age of sixty-one had, by "hook or crook," acquired a sizable plantation of broad, cultivated acres, deep wooded areas and rich pasturelands. The Joe McCullough plantation was set up with a dwelling of more than average spaciousness, a row of small dwellings known as slave quarters, two barns with stables, a carriage house, a wagon shed, a corncrib, a smokehouse, a blacksmith shop, a gristmill, a cotton gin and a country store. The more than average spacious dwelling, in which Joe and his family lived, was called "the big house" by the group of slaves who served as household servants, stable boys and farm laborers. Joe could not be classed with the landed gentry of the coast, but with his landed holdings and numerous slaves, he played the part of a country gentleman and a shrewd businessman.

The store was his greatest asset. He had a monopoly on the community trade. His was the only store in a large rural area, and from it and at his own price, he sold everything from imported colored silks for ladies' fine dresses to handmade bolts for farmers' crude plows. In addition to this, it was a stop for the stagecoaches that plied between Augusta, Georgia, at the head of navigation on the Savannah River, and Asheville, North Carolina, at the end of a land trade route on top of the Blue Ridge Mountains. All in all, it was a rendezvous for the neighborhood farmers.

These farmers belonged neither to the highest nor the lowest strata of society, wealth or education. They were the good, hard, sturdy middle class, who owned small farms, a few slaves and log buildings. Their education did not go far beyond the three Rs, and they kept in touch with the belated news from the outside world by the bimonthly newspapers that were passed around from house to house. On Saturday afternoon, they were wont to meet at Joe's store and freely, loudly and often hotly discuss local gossip, current events and politics. It was not hard for the discussions on their favorite subjects to reach the boiling point while the hair would rise and the tobacco juice would fly.

It was a Saturday afternoon, and Joe was very busy. A number of customers came in and went out. A number of loafers sat around the fire. Jerry Wilson was not so much of a customer as he was a loafer, but for some reason he was late claiming his seat in the loafers' council. As he entered the store, he said, in a bantering tone, "Howdy, Uncle Joe, where is your grindstone? I have an axe to grind."

Uncle Joe paused, peered over his spectacles, shrugged his shoulders and said, "Humph," in a rather disgusted tone and turned back to serving his customer.

"Come on, Uncle Joe, tell us where 'tis. You wouldn't mind a neighbor using it, would you?" said John Berry, who had followed along with Jerry.

Uncle Joe paused and again peered over his spectacles, grinned shrewdly and said, "By faith, ye are welcome to use me grindstone, but first ye must find it."

"What's the joke about the grindstone?" asked Tom Donald after Jerry and John had settled themselves in the loafers' circle.

"Haven't you heard about Uncle Joe's fine new grindstone?" laughed John. "No," said Tom, and the entire group turned a look of inquiry toward John. "Tell us about it," continued Tom. "You tell 'em, Jerry."

Jerry spat and drew his hand across his mouth and began. "Wald you know Uncle Joe bought most of Widow Carson's stuff t'other day, and in it wuz a good-looking grindstone, but when it comes to using it—it twarn't no good. It had done like Old Joe does lots of times—it had lost its temper. You could grind an axe from now 'til doomsday and never get an edge on it." The crowd laughed, and Tom said, "I can't believe Old Joe got tricked in a trade. His years have started telling on him."

"If he did, I guarantee you he will trick somebody else in the same way and mount be one o' us. We had better keep our eyes skinned," said Douglas Connelly, "or we'll get skinned." All laughed again and arose to meet the stagecoach as it rolled in from Augusta.

The stagecoach deposited its passengers and the mail. The mail was separated, and customers and loafers turned their steps homeward. Left alone, Old Joe covered the dying embers on the hearth with ashes, closed the store for the day and prepared to turn in for the night. On the porch of the store, he paused, lifted his chest and chuckled to himself. "Yes, anybody that can find that darned grindstone is welcome to use it. Joe McCullough never comes out at the 'little end of the horn,'" and looking toward a wagon that was loaded with three bales of lint cotton, which were to be carried to Augusta on Monday to be sold, he continued his musing. "Yes, there are plenty of 'tricks in trade,' and Joe knows 'em all."

As a matter of fact, the lost-tempered grindstone was securely packed in the center of one of the three-hundred-pound bales of lint, and in Augusta, Joe thought to himself, it would be weighed and sold as cotton. He also thought the cotton would be put into a warehouse and then perhaps be shipped to a mill in England or Ireland to be woven into cloth.

In these processes, he thought, it would lose its identity as a bale sold by Joe McCullough, and that would be the last, so far as he was concerned, of the lost-tempered grindstone.

With this in mind, he stopped by the wagon, patted the grindstone bale of cotton and again chuckled to himself. "Who knows but what one of my friends in the auld countree may fall heir to this masterpiece of strategy."

Winter passed, the grindstone episode was forgotten and the spring with its routine activities came. In the community church, it was customary to celebrate the Lord's Supper on the second Sunday in May. On the Saturday preceding this service, a preparatory service was held. Here, one repented of his or her sins and shortcomings, begged forgiveness and made themselves worthy to partake of the Supper.

It was now Saturday before the second Sunday in May 1852. Allen Chandler, a good deacon in the church, was dressing to attend the preparatory service. "Allen," said Temperance, his wife, "as you pass Joe McCullough's store, get five pounds of sugar—and watch Old Joe when he weighs it, and see that he gives you five pounds." "You don't think he would cheat me, do you?" "No, I don't think so—I know it."

Most of the people in the neighborhood, including Joe McCullough, were present at the service, and the preacher waxed long, loud and eloquent on the text: "Your sins will find you out." Joe, being a pillar in the church, sat at the right of the pulpit in the "amen corner," and as the preacher uttered truths of righteousness or pronounced curses of condemnation, Joe would portray his accord with the sentiment by a nod of the head and a muffled "A-men." When the collection hat was passed, his contribution was conspicuous but not too generous.

After the service, Joe hurried home to open the store for the purpose of accommodating any customer who, as they returned from church, might want to make purchases. After Joe, Allen Chandler was the first of the church attendants to reach the store. In they went, and Allen asked for the five pounds of sugar. "Allen," said Joe, "the bin is empty, but the wagon has just come in from Augusta, and on it is a whole barrel." So, Joe sent for the cask.

By this time, others returning from the church had stopped by the store. The ladies went on the inside to do small shopping, and Joe busied himself with them. The men, who were the regular Saturday afternoon customers and loafers, lingered on the outside to talk and to watch the barrel of sugar come off the wagon and onto the porch of the store. The barrel was made of thick boards and was well constructed. The implements for removing the head were crude. Forcing the head was almost impossible, and different men offered suggestions. Finally, when quite a crowd had gathered to watch the operation, a heavy stroke with an axe splintered the head, and bits of slivered timbers fell into the sugar. As the sugar was cleaned, a hard, gray object appeared.

All talking ceased. The crowd gathered closer around the barrel. For a few seconds, there was a death of silence—then Alex Wakefield said, "I'll swear," and burst into a roar of laughter and was joined by others as a full understanding of the situation burst upon them.

"Who'd a thought it," cried Tom Connelly. "The boomerang has returned," said Jerry Wilson. "The dove couldn't find a place for her foot," said John Berry.

With each witticism, the laughter grew louder and more convulsive—hands were clasped, knees bent and bodies doubled. Hearing the ruckus, Joe moved toward the door.

He briskly, proudly and courteously strutted onto the porch with an air of one who feels himself capable of coping with any and every situation. He had nearly reached the barrel when he suddenly stopped and stood rooted in his tracks. His eyes bulged, his mouth opened, he caught his breath and over his fat bespectacled face spread crimson consternation, anger, embarrassment and humiliation.

Sure enough, before his own eyes and in the presence of customers and loafers, his sins had found him out. Fully exposed on top of the barrel of sugar there lay the lost-tempered grindstone that the shrewd Joe McCullough, who knew all the tricks in trade, had sold in soft, white cotton and had unwittingly rebought in glistening white sugar.

Laughter became boisterous. Joe was half-turned as if to reenter the store when his Irish wit asserted itself. He sensed the humor in his defeat—realized that others, too, knew tricks in the trade. So, he faced the barrel again, removed his spectacles, threw back his head, burst into ringing laughter and exclaimed, "Oh, begory, it looks damn familiar!"

Editor's note: The cotton sold for ten cents per pound. The sugar was bought for seven cents per pound.

MEETING STREET FEUD

The Logue and Timmerman Feud in Edgefield County, South Carolina
By Jim Scott

In a small farming community known as Meeting Street in northern Edgefield County near the present-day U.S. Highway 25 there was a family known as the Logues who had lived in the area for several generations. They farmed cotton, wheat, oats and corn and had cattle, horses and mules. They also had a sawmill. Over the years, they had made a good living and acquired a lot of land, timber, farmland and a lot of pastureland. They were also known for their ability to train hunting dogs and had bird dogs, beagles and hounds. During the hunting seasons, many hunters from far and wide would come and stay at the Logue house and enjoy hunting quail, rabbit and fox for several days at a time.

There were several members of the Logue family. I will not mention all; there were George, Joe and Wallace. George was a veteran of World War I, came home and remained a bachelor. He lived in the home with his brother Wallace, who was married to Sue Logue. The other brother was Joe, who was married and lived nearby. He had a son named Joe Frank.

In the late 1920s or early 1930s, a small farm near the Logues' came up for sale. There was a store building on this property, and the property sold quickly to a Mr. Davis Timmerman, who opened the store and farmed part time. The Timmerman family became very active in the Meeting Street community and in the school and church; Davis was elected to the school board.

During this period, South Carolina passed education laws requiring that schoolteachers must have a college education and a South Carolina teacher's certificate. Mrs. Sue Logue was and had been the teacher at the Meeting Street school and was educated well but did not have a formal college degree. This was a problem for the school. Mr. Davis Timmerman, the school board chairman, hired a new schoolteacher since Mrs. Logue was disqualified by the new law. This action infuriated the Logue family to a point of rage. Sue Logue went to Edgefield to see the Edgefield superintendent of education, who just happened to be J. Strom Thurman (later to become judge, World War II hero, governor and U.S. senator for many terms). After this meeting, Mrs. Sue Logue retained her job as the teacher at the Meeting Street school— kind of like the scene in the *Forrest Gump* movie. Then Mr. Timmerman had to let the new teacher go, with egg all over his face. This caused contention between the Logues and Timmermans that was never forgotten.

There was a tenant farmer who was shot and killed in the community. There was an inquest and a trial on this death, and the Logues and Timmermans were on different sides again. This caused yet more contention between the two families.

One day, one of the Logues' calves got into Mr. Timmerman's pasture, and somehow Mr. Timmerman's mule kicked and killed the calf. Wallace Logue demanded restitution, and an agreement to the amount was made. The next morning, Wallace went to Mr. Timmerman's store for the money, and an argument started over the amount of restitution to be paid. Wallace got an axe handle out of a barrel in the store and attempted to hit Mr. Timmerman. Mr. Timmerman pulled his gun and killed Wallace Logue. Mr. Timmerman was acquitted on self-defense, and the Logues went into a rage.

George and Sue Logue visited their nephew Joe Frank Logue, who was a police sergeant in Spartanburg, South Carolina. They asked him to find someone to kill Davis Timmerman and would pay $500 for the assassination. Joe Frank refused. A couple of months later, Joe Frank met Clarence Bagwell, who lived with the madam of a brothel on Asheville Highway in Spartanburg. Joe Frank asked Clarence if he would kill a man in Edgefield for $500. Clarence told Joe Frank that he would kill every person who lived in Edgefield for $500. Joe Frank knew he had his man. Joe Frank got in touch with his Uncle George and Aunt Sue, and they gave him the money. Joe Frank drove Clarence Bagwell to Mr. Timmerman's store one day. Clarence got out of the car, and Joe Frank drove off a short distance. He turned around to come back for Clarence. Clarence got back into the car and told Joe Frank that the deed was done. Joe Frank paid Clarence the money, and they drove back to Spartanburg.

The next day, the two drove to Tryon, North Carolina, and threw the gun into Lake Lanier. On the way back, they stopped at a bar to get some beer. They met a lovely girl who worked at the bar. After that day, Clarence and the girl at the bar became lovers. Clarence had $500, which was a lot of money in 1941. The woman who Clarence lived with in Spartanburg found out about the affair several months later.

Meanwhile, a manhunt was on for the murderer of Davis Timmerman in Edgefield. Suspects from as far away as Arkansas were brought in for questioning. The leads led to nothing, but it was all far from over.

In the meantime, the lady with whom Clarence Bagwell was living went to visit the sheriff of Spartanburg County and inquired about a murder in Edgefield some months past. The sheriff got her name and address but had no information for her at the time. The next day, he contacted the sheriff of Edgefield and found out about the murder.

The Spartanburg sheriff visited the lady and took Clarence Bagwell in for questioning. Ole Clarence just spilled it all and fingered Joe Frank for the planning of the murder. Joe Frank was on duty at the Spartanburg City Police Department that night. The Spartanburg sheriff brought Joe Frank in for questioning and called in South Carolina Law Enforcement Division (SLED) officers who immediately took Joe Frank and Clarence Bagwell into custody. They took them to the Central Correctional Institute (CCI) in Columbia, South Carolina, where they questioned them further. A warrant was issued for George and Sue Logue and was to be served the next morning. This was leaked to George and Sue, so they got a sharecropper named Mr. Dorn to come to the house and help them resist arrest. The next day, when the sheriff of Edgefield County arrived to serve the warrant, a shootout began. One of the deputies and Mr. Dorn were mortally wounded. The police surrounded the house. The district judge, who just happened to be the Honorable J. Strom Thurmond, was summoned to the house. While there, he was able to get the guns away from George and Sue Logue.

George and Sue Logue were tried along with Clarence Bagwell, and they all received the death penalty. They were executed in 1941 at the Central Correctional Institute in Columbia. Joe Frank, who was tried separately, received a life sentence. While serving this sentence, he became a trusty, enabling him to train and run the hounds. These hounds were used by SLED to track escaped prisoners and criminals. In doing so, Joe Frank actually became a folk hero. Don't believe it? Google it.

WARE PLACE CROSSROADS

By Jim Scott

Mrs. Ellen Charles Woodside and Her Family of Woodville, South Carolina, on the Old Augusta Road

Ellen Permelia Charles was born to Israel Charles and Permelia Sullivan on February 13, 1838. She was the third of eight children. They first lived in a house on the old road from Ware Place to Pelzer, South Carolina, and later moved to the old Israel Charles house, a two-story house at the corner of Augusta Road and Garrison Road called the Four Chimney House.

In 1857, Ellen married Dr. John Lawrence Woodside. They made their home in what is now known as Woodville, which is about two miles north of Ware Place on the Augusta Road. Dr. Woodside was from the Fairview community a little south and west of Fountain Inn, South Carolina. Ellen and Dr. John attended Fairview Presbyterian Church for many years. In 1882, Mrs. Ellen Woodside founded Lickville Presbyterian Church on property donated by W.A. McKelvey on the Augusta Road about two miles south of Ware Place.

Dr. John and Ellen had thirteen children, four of whom became very successful in the cotton manufacturing industry. They had mills in Greenville, Simpsonville and Fountain Inn. The Woodside Mill in Greenville was known as the largest mill under one roof in the world. The four brothers bought thousands of beachfront acres at Myrtle Beach, South Carolina, and built the famous Ocean Forrest Hotel on the beach. They started the development of Myrtle Beach and built an eighteen-hole golf course, which was completed in 1929. They also were in the banking business, with banks in Woodville, Taylors and headquarters in Greenville in a seventeen-story skyscraper, and they built the Poinsett Hotel across the street. The Woodsides also gave the land and lots of financial support to the new Ellen Woodside High School in Woodville and furnished a building for a temporary school until the modern two-story structure was completed in 1925.

Tragically, the stock market crash of 1929 destroyed the Woodside empire, and by 1935, all of the holdings had been lost. Today, there are no Woodsides living in Woodville, only some of the edifices they built and left behind.

The Ware Family of Abbeville and Greenville Counties

The Ware family came from Caroline County, Virginia, in the late sixteenth century and settled in Abbeville County on the Saluda River. Edmund Ware married his second wife, Peggy Gaines, after arriving in South Carolina, and they had eight children.

Edmund became a general in the South Carolina militia early in the seventeenth century and owned a large plantation on the Saluda River where he was granted a permit by the South Carolina legislature to build a toll bridge across the Saluda to Laurens County. Later, Edmund built a huge mill lower down the Saluda River on a large shoal near current-day Ware Shoals. This mill consisted of two turbines, one a horizontal wheel at the entrance into the canal for small horsepower work and the large one at the end of the canal, which was a huge water wheel to produce a lot of horsepower to drive a gin or sawmill. His wife's family, the Gaineses, built a mill directly across the river on the Laurens County side called Gaines Mill. We are told that the Ware and Gaines families had an agreement that if an incorporated town were to come to this place, it would be called Gainesville. In 1909, Thomas Riegel came in and bought the Abbeville County (now Greenwood County) side of the Saluda River. He put up a huge textile plant on the property and named the town Ware Shoals.

The Ware and Gaines families prospered from their enterprises, especially the Wares, who became very rich and had a lot of influence in this area of the state.

One of Edmund's and Peggy's sons, Thomas Edwin Ware, born in 1806, was married to a Miss Mary Williams Jones, who lived on the Jones/Williams plantation that was owned by Mary's father, Captain Adam Jones, and her mother, Jane Williams Jones. The Joneses inherited a large plantation from Jane's parents, who had received a grant for 1,700 acres in the area now called Ware Place. Captain Jones had built a large beautiful two-story frame house on the crossroads of the Augusta Road and the old road now called the Pelzer Road. This house is still standing today.

The Wares lived in the big house with Captain and Mrs. Jones, and Thomas Ware ran the plantation and was very successful. He became an active politician and was elected to three terms in the South Carolina House of Representatives in the 1840s and was appointed to several high offices, one giving him the title of colonel.

In the early 1850s, Mrs. Jones died, and Mary became the mistress of the home. Captain Jones was getting old and became very mean to his daughter Mary at times. As time went on, Captain Jones grew worse in his abuse to his daughter to the point that the Wares decided to leave Ware Place and move to Greenville. When they had moved all of their belongings, Mary was in the carriage and Colonel Ware was in the house talking to Captain Jones. Captain Jones went into a rage and grabbed a fire poker from near the fireplace and started beating Colonel Ware, breaking his arm with the blows aimed at his head. Colonel Ware was able to get a pistol from his pocket and shot Captain Jones several times and killed him.

Colonel Ware was charged with and convicted of manslaughter in April 1853. He served just a few days and was pardoned by his friend and governor of South Carolina, Governor John Lawrence Manning.

The Wares lived in Greenville and were very prosperous until Colonel Ware's death in 1873. The colonel and his wife, Mary, along with the Joneses and several of their immediate family, are interred in the Ware family cemetery close to the house called Ware Place.

Thomas E. Ware Jr. lived in the house until his death in 1904. The house is still in possession of the family who purchased it from the Ware family. It stands at the intersection of U.S. 25 and Highway 8.

THE KINGDOM OF HAPPY LAND

Summarized from the text by Sadie Smathers Patton, 1957, and the articles of Mike Hembree in the *Greenville News*, 1987

The Kingdom of Happy Land existed in the Blue Ridge Mountains of North and South Carolina during the later portion of the 1800s following the War Between the States. The 180-acre communal village was formed by ex-slaves looking for a better life together as an extended family of sorts. From interviews of folks who remembered it themselves or from stories they were told, these families came to the area of Tuxedo, North Carolina, about 1864 or 1865 from Mississippi looking for a land of new happiness. Walking along the trails, their leader enticed others to join them, and when they came to a nearly vacated plantation along the drover's road from Asheville to Greenville, they found a respite. This plantation's slave cabins were now vacant, and the widowed owner and her widowed son were trying to carry on with the inn and camp they had been running for years along the Saluda Gap Road.

Serepta Merritt Davis and her son, Tom, whose wife was Sarah Goodwin, were from families who had been innkeepers along the Gap Road for many years. Serepta's father, for whom Merrittsville at the base of the Saluda Gap in South Carolina was named, kept a drover's camp and inn there even before she was born. Sarah Goodwin's father did the same, also running the toll stop at the base of the Gap. They had just moved up the mountain, and Serepta's husband, Col. Davis, owned a plantation that went on for miles crossing the area on the state lines.

So, the group of weary travelers moved into the Davises' cabins and set about reviving the farm lands and making their own village. They worked and collected and shared all the funds to support themselves under the guidance of their "King and Queen." The names of these first two have been lost, but they led the colony to maintain the camp and inn and hired out to locals for various jobs so that by 1882 they owned 180 acres straddling the state line.

When the stories of the Kingdom were recorded after 1950, the forty-year experiment had been disassembled for half a century. But children of the Kingdom remembered their childhood there and how their families entered into this group. Ezel Couch was brought to the mountain from Cross Anchor, SC, in 1873 as a one-year-old by his parents, George and Maggie. Ezel soon had two siblings, Anderson and Mary. Their parents were former slaves following the advice of a Reverend Ezel who traveled through Newberry, Union, Enoree, Cross Anchor, Spartanburg and other Upstate South Carolina towns. Many of his congregations' people came to the Kingdom and joined the colony in Happy Land.

This group increased the colony to somewhere between 200 and 300 members. Two from Enoree were Harold Whitmire and his wife, Hannah, and their family. Then there were Wiley and Rachel Bennett from Cross Anchor, William Montgomery and Louella with her two brothers, Ambrose and Henry Bobo, from Spartanburg County, and there was Jerry Casey. One important member of the Montgomery family, Robert, joined the group as well. He and his sister-in-law, Louella, soon became the "King and Queen," taking care of the colony of the Kingdom of Happy Land until it finally dispersed about 1900.

On the state line between the homes of the King and the Queen was a chapel for religious services and classes for the children where Louella trained the students in a kind of Sunday School. She taught religion, reading, and singing—spirituals, hymns and other songs. Her choir would travel throughout Tuxedo to black and white communities sharing their voices as they went from home to home on summer evenings. Older students went to school near Hendersonville at a place called Possum Hollow and were taught by Rev. Walter Allen.

After working the farm and drover's stands for years, the group members began to see the decline of travel on the road. Although they and some others continued moving their farm products into South Carolina, many of the droves of animals were being transported on trains and need for the food products they sold to the drovers was diminishing. Various families moved on to other areas of North Carolina when the colony of Happy Land began to break up. Some went to Sylva to work in the mica mines, while others found opportunities in Hendersonville. The last member of the group, Jerry Casey, died there in 1918.

Remnants of the Kingdom can still be found in road names near the state line along the Old U.S. 25 and along the Green River. This vital group should be remembered as a stabilizing force in Tuxedo and Flat Rock for nearly half a century.

HOT SPRINGS AND JEWEL HILL

By the end of the summer of 2019, the authors had done most of the stomping, as Jim calls our field research. We had started searching for deep cuts in the woods along the roads and keeping our eyes open for concrete left unpaved along U.S. 25 in South Carolina. We were novices in this type of research. Jim and I both depended on help from friends and ancient maps and aerials that were very current. But the best part was talking with locals we ran into along the way.

Then in the spring of 2020, we decided to turn our stomping into this text, and we wanted to include North Carolina's Buncombe Turnpike. So, we had to move into active research with a pandemic going on in the world. We decided to start in Hot Springs, and on a day reminiscent of January, the search for concrete on the mountain turned into a wet, dreary, chilly venture. When we reached the village, I remembered being there before for a U.S. 25 yard sale several years ago with another special friend.

Hot Springs is a small, historic town on the Appalachian Trail with beautiful nineteenth-century homes and a turn-of-the-century brick downtown. The railroad and the French Broad River pass through the town, and Buncombe Turnpike is part of the history. Jim, Cathy Morton and I passed on to the Tennessee line searching for concrete sections of the Dixie Highway. A benefit of this search was finding several wonderful sights along the way, such as the bridge and railroad track just over the line in Tennessee, the quaint church backing up to a meadow with a mountain view and a dirt road leading to an unusual barn and private road. Taking any road in this area brings wonderful surprises.

Then, back in town, nothing much was open to anyone. But the outdoor store for hikers on the AT was and had a great little display of local books—just what this reader/writer needed. So, I walked away with several, to the benefit of this history of a road. We did not find any restrooms open at all though, so we decided to move on back toward Marshall. On the way we were trying to follow those side roads and stumbled onto Walnut, alias

Jewel Hill, the first area courthouse in a log cabin, now a lovely church on a hill surrounded by an ancient cemetery (and I mean surrounded). As we looked for more information, Jim stopped at a local business and found a young historian who shared the history of the courthouse/church and showed us the cemetery and its historical signs. In spite of the virus, you took us in, and we want to thank you, Andrew, for taking on strangers and sharing your love of your place.

NOTES

Background Information

1. Bishop Francis Asbury, *Journal of Rev. Francis Asbury*, Vol. III (New York: Lane and Scott, 1852), October 24, 1801, 39.

Chapter 1

2. John H. Logan, *A History of the Upper Country of South Carolina*, Vol. 1 (Charleston, SC: S.G. Courtney and Co., 1859), 12–15.
3. Ibid., 16.
4. George Ellison, "Where the Buffalo Roam," *Smoky Mountain News*, November 10, 2010, smokymountainnews.com/news/item/2478-where-the-buffalo-roam.
5. Taylor Barnhill, "Ancient Road Infrastructure Created by Bison," The Laurel of Asheville, 2017, thelaurelofasheville.com/lifestyle/heritage/ancient-road-infrastructure-created-bison.
6. John Preston Arthur, *Western North Carolina, A History* (Asheville, NC: Edward Buncombe Chapter of the Daughters of the American Revolution, 1914), 250–51.
7. Arthur, *Western North Carolina*, 229.
8. Ibid., 18.
9. Logan, *History of the Upper Country of South Carolina*, 15–16.

10. Barnhill, "Ancient Road Infrastructure."
11. Arthur, *Western North Carolina*, 229.
12. James M. Richardson, *History of Greenville County, South Carolina* (Greenville, SC: Southern Historical Press, 1930), 18.
13. Margaret Watson, *Greenwood County Sketches* (Greenwood, SC: Attic Press, Inc., 1970), 2.
14. Ron Barnett, "Historic Cherokee Path Route Discovered in Six Mile," *Greenville News*, October 6, 2016.
15. Arthur, *Western North Carolina*, 230.
16. George Estes, "Ware Shoals History," interview by Anne Peden, spring 2019.
17. Arthur, *Western North Carolina*, 18–19; Will Chavez, "Cherokee Phoenix Ancestors Remained East for Various Reasons," March 25, 2016, www.cherokeephoenix.org/Article/index/10143.
18. Watson, *Greenwood County Sketches*, 2.
19. Arthur, *Western North Carolina*, 230.
20. Watson, *Greenwood County Sketches*, 35.
21. Logan, *History of the Upper Country of South Carolina*, 315.
22. Ibid., 192–203.
23. Richardson, *History of Greenville County*, 21.
24. "Alexander McGillivray," Wikipedia.
25. Richardson, *History of Greenville County*, 21.
26. Workers of the Writers' Program of the Work Projects Administration, SC, *Palmetto Place Names* (n.p.: SC Education Association, n.d.), 39.
27. Logan, *History of the Upper Country of South Carolina*, 249.
28. Ibid., 250–51.
29. Ibid., 251–52.
30. Logan, *History of the Upper Country of South Carolina*, 52.
31. Richardson, *History of Greenville County*, 23.
32. Ibid., 22–23.
33. Watson, *Greenwood County Sketches*, 4–5.
34. Richardson, *History of Greenville County*, 23.
35. Ibid., 24.
36. John Abney Chapman, *History of Edgefield County from Earliest Settlement* (Newberry, SC: Elbert H. Aull, Publisher and Printer, 1897), 22.
37. Ibid., 20.
38. Ibid.
39. Watson, *Greenwood County Sketches*, 10–12.
40. Ibid., 31.

41. Ibid., 8–11.

42. Arthur, *Western North Carolina*, 81.

43. Ibid., 89, 232.

44. Chapman, *History of Edgefield County from the Earliest Settlement*, 16.

45. Richardson, *History of Greenville County*, 32–33.

46. Ibid., 32–34.

47. Kenneth E. Sassaman, *Early Pottery in the Southeast* (Tuscaloosa: University of Alabama Press), 46.

Chapter 2

48. Mann Batson, *Early Travel and Accommodations Along the Roads of the Upper Part of Greenville County, South Carolina* (Greenville, SC: Greenville Literacy Association, 1995), 51–66.

49. David Duncan Wallace, *South Carolina: A Short History, 1520–1948* (Columbia: University of South Carolina Press, 1951), 557–68.

50. Richardson, *History of Greenville County*, 49, 53–54.

51. Arthur, *Western North Carolina*, 114, 132–34, 144–45.

52. "Buncombe County History," Wikipedia.

53. "Trail of Tears," Wikipedia.

54. Arthur, *Western North Carolina*, 230.

55. Ibid., 229.

56. Asbury, *Journal*, Vol. II, November 6, 1800, 481.

57. Ibid., Vol. III, November 3, 1802, 90.

58. Ibid., Vol. III, October 24, 1803, 133.

59. Arthur, *Western North Carolina*, 233–34.

60. Ibid., 230–31.

61. Ibid., 236.; Archie Vernon Huff, *Greenville: A History of a City and County in the South Carolina Piedmont* (Columbia: University of South Carolina Press, 1995), 64.

62. Huff, *Greenville*, 86–87.

63. Ibid., 87–88.

64. Arthur, *Western North Carolina*, 237.

65. "French Broad River," Wikipedia.

66. Della Hazel Moore, *Hot Springs of North Carolina* (Johnson City, TN: Overmountain Press, 1992), 15, 18.

67. Ibid., 33–34.

68. Ibid., 55, 57, 88–89.

69. "Mountain Dew," *Asheville Citizen-Times*, October 26, 1930.

70. Asbury, *Journal*, Vol. III, November 8,1802.

71. Fork Shoals Historical Society, *Fork Shoals* (Charleston, SC: Arcadia Press, 2012), 101–3.

72. Chapman, *History of Edgefield County from the Earliest Settlement*, 5.

73. Bettis Rainsford, *The Story of the Pine House* (Edgefield, SC: Rainsford, 2013), 1–6.

74. Nancy Mims, *The Old Stage Road* (n.p.: Edgefield Advertiser, 1976; reprinted 2009, Judith Russell), 9–13.

75. Bettis Rainsford, *The Early History of Horns Creek Baptist Church* (Edgefield, SC: Rainsford, 2014), 3.

76. Mims, *Old Stage Road*, 12–13.

77. Chapman, *History of Edgefield County from the Earliest Settlement*, 20.

Chapter 3

78. Batson, *Early Travel and Accommodations*, 53.

79. Ibid., 38–41.

80. Moore, *Hot Springs of North Carolina*, 18–19.

81. Ibid., 57–64, 68.

82. George B. Ellenberg, *Mule South to Tractor South* (Tuscaloosa: University of Alabama Press, 2007), 33.

83. Ibid., 54–74.

84. Ibid., 41–53.

85. Batson, *Early Travel and Accommodations*, 47–49, 68–69.

86. Ibid., 40–44.

87. Richardson, *History of Greenville County*, 63.

88. Huff, *Greenville*, 89–91.

89. Arthur, *Western North Carolina*, 381.

90. S.S. Crittenden, *The Greenville Century Book, 1903* (Greenville, SC: Press of the Greenville News, 1903), 44–45.

91. Arthur, *Western North Carolina*, 502.

92. Crittenden, *Greenville Century Book*, 45.

93. Frances Causey, *The Long Shadow*, PBS movie, 2017.

94. Caroline Coleman, "Where Hospitality Abounds," newspaper clipping with no publisher or date, circa 1940s.

95. Anne Peden, *Holly Spring African American School* (Columbia: South Carolina State Historic Preservation Office, 2019), section 8, page 11.

96. Gretchen Sorin, *Driving While Black* (New York: Liveright Publishing Corporation, 2020), 4.

97. Leonard Todd, *Carolina Clay, The Like and Legend of the Slave Potter, Dave* (New York: W.W. Norton & Company, 2008), 68–75.

98. Sorin, *Driving While Black*, 6–10.

99. G. Walton Williams, *The Best Friend* (Dunwoody, GA: Norman S. Berg Publisher, 1969), cover.

100. Ibid.

101. Ray Belcher, *Greenville County, South Carolina: From Cotton Fields to Textile Center of the World* (Charleston, SC: The History Press, 2006), 15–20.

102. Fork Shoals Historical Society, *Fork Shoals*, 66.

103. Francis Walker, *Tenth Census, Water Power of the United States* (Washington, D.C.: Census Office, 1880).

104. John R. Stilgoe, *Common Landscape of America, 1580–1845*, Google Books; William S. Brockington Jr., "Transportation," University of South Carolina, June 28, 2016, www.scencyclopedia.org/sce/entries/transportation; Troy L. Kickler, "Plank Roads," northcarolinahistory.org/encyclopedia/plank-roads.

105. John Hammond Moore, *The South Carolina Highway Department, 1917–1987* (Columbia: University of South Carolina Press, 1987), 15.

106. Kickler, "Plank Roads."

107. Stilgoe, *Common Landscape of America.*

108. "Plank Roads," *Asheville Citizen-Times*, January 18, 1987.

109. "Our Plank Roads," *Edgefield Advertiser*, November 30, 1853.

110. Arthur, *Western North Carolina*, 253.

111. Ibid., 249.

112. Batson, *Early Travel and Accommodations*, 76.

113. Wallace, *South Carolina*, 376.

114. Moore, *South Carolina Highway Department*, 14.

Chapter 4

115. Batson, *Early Travel and Accommodations*, 9.

116. Crittenden, *Greenville Century Book*, 65–68.; Bonnes Amies Club, *Piedmont* (Charleston, SC: Arcadia Publishing Company, 2014), 39–54.

117. Crittenden, *Greenville Century Book*, 68–70; Belcher, *Greenville County*, 29–51; Kelly L. Odom, *Greenville Textiles* (Charleston, SC: Arcadia Publishing Company, 2015), 9–50.

118. "Greenville, Knoxville, and Western Railroad," Wikipedia; Henry Poor, *Poor's Manual of the Railroads of the United States*, Vol. 22, 1029, Google Books.

119. Watson, *Greenwood County Sketches*, 222–23.

120. Frank Woods and Mann McNinch, *From Hill to Dale to Hollow* (Columbia, SC: R.L. Bryan and Company, 1983), 1.

Chapter 5

121. Tammy Ingram, *Dixie Highway* (Chapel Hill: University of North Carolina Press, 2014), 8.

122. Ibid., 8.

123. Ibid., 6, 31–32.

124. "Southern Cotton Mills," *St. Louis Globe-Democrat*, April 24, 1987, Newspapers.com.

125. "Asbury Churchill Latimer," Wikipedia, 2020.

126. Howard Lawrence Preston, *Dirt Roads to Dixie* (Knoxville: University of Tennessee Press, 1991), 19.

127. Ibid., 33.

128. "National Bodies Open Conventions in Textile Hall," *Greenville Civic and Commercial Journal* 2, no. 6 (April 1923).

129. "Bankhead Route," *Greenville Civic and Commercial Journal* (November 1922): 13.

130. Ellenberg, *Mule South to Tractor South*, 31–36, 100–1.

131. Ibid., 100–1.

132. Ibid.

Chapter 6

133. Ingram, *Dixie Highway*, 43–52.

134. Ibid., 75–78.

135. Robert Yost and Patricia Yost, *Late to the Party in the Roaring '20s,* (Palm Beach, FL: Pineapple Press, Inc., 2020), 5–7.

136. Ibid., 81–85, 119.

137. Ibid., 119–21.

138. Sorin, *Driving While Black*, 17.

139. Ibid., 12.

140. Ibid.

141. Victor H. Green with notes by Nat Gertler, *The Negro Motorist Green Book Compendium* (Camarillo, CA: About Comics, 2019), 74, 104, 113, 148.

142. Anne Peden, Greenville County Historic Preservation Commission work.

143. Ingram, *Dixie Highway*, 52–56.

144. Ibid., 5.

145. "Over Half Done," *Greenville News*, June 21, 1927, Newspapers.com.

146. Site #4, this document of a concrete bridge dated 1910 on the Old Buncombe Road between Greenville and Travelers Rest.

147. "Augusta St. Paving Nearly Completed," *Greenville News*, November 4, 1911, Newspapers.com.

148. "Accomplishments of the Chamber of Commerce," *Asheville Citizen-Times*, December 24, 1922, www.newspapers.com/image/200088070/?terms=asheville%2Bdixie.

149. Judy Bainbridge, "The Legacy of W.G., the 'Other Sirrine,'" *Greenville News*, August 13, 2020, D1.

150. Ingram, *Dixie Highway*, 105.

Chapter 7

151. Ultimate History Project, "Out for a Drive: Motoring Clothes for the New Automobile," ultimatehistoryproject.com/early-20th-century-motoring-clothes.html.

152. Ingram, *Dixie Highway*, 155.

153. Joshua Beau Blackwell, *Used to Be a Rough Place in Them Hills: Moonshine, the Dark Corner, and the New South* (Bloomington, IN: AuthorHouse, 2009), 53–70.

154. Ibid., 10–14.

155. Dean Campbell, *Twice-Told Tales of the Dark Corner* (Landrum, SC: Tarmaczar Productions), 77–78.

156. Blackwell, *Used to Be a Rough Place*, 57–61.

157. Ingram, *Dixie Highway*, 6.

158. Blackwell, *Used to Be a Rough Place*, 70–72.

159. Ibid., 97–99.

160. Ingram, *Dixie Highway*, 197–98.

161. "Dixie Highway Secession," *Aiken Standard*, July 27, 1927, Newspapers.com.

162. "Silas Trowbridge Notebook," 1904, Greenville County Library, Trowbridge Collection.

163. Ingram, *Dixie Highway*, 198.

164. Sorin, *Driving While Black*, 267.

165. Ibid., 197–98.

166. "Asbury Churchill Latimer," SC Encyclopedia.org, www.scencyclopedia. org/sce/entries/latimer-asbury-churchwell.

167. "Dixie Highway Taxes and Bonds," *Augusta Advertizer*, August 25, 1920, Newspapers.com.

168. "Concrete Prices and Places," *Greenwood Journal*, May 17, 1921, Newspapers.com.

169. "Road Construction and Bonds," *Edgefield Advertizer*, August 25, 1920, Newspapers.com.

170. Wallace, *South Carolina*, 680.

171. "Rhett Plan," *Manning Times*, January 8, 1919, Newspapers.com.

Chapter 8

172. Ingram, *Dixie Highway*, 196–97.

173. "Dixie Highway Secession," *Aiken Standard*, July 27, 1927, Newspapers. com.

174. South Carolina Department of Transportation, Plans Online, March 3, 2020, falcon.scdot.org/falconwebv3/default.aspx.

175. "Paving the Dixie," *Greenville News*, November 8, 1928, Newspapers.com.

176. "Tourists in Florida Deeply Interested," *Asheville Citizen-Times*, March 16, 1925.

177. "Local Motor Club Distributes Maps," *Asheville Citizen-Times*, January 13, 1925.

178. David Southern, "Highways," NCPEDIA, www.ncpedia.org/highways-part-2-north-carolinas.

179. "Railroad to Be Built in Paving Augusta Road to Laurens County," *Greenville News*, September 24, 1927, Newspapers.com.

180. Ben Knight, "Stories of the Road," interview by Anne Peden and Jim Scott, August 2019.

181. "Ben Sawyer, SC Chief Highway Commissioner," *Charlotte Observer*, November 22, 1930, Newspapers.com.

182. Wallace, *South Carolina*, 682.

183. Preston, *Dirt Roads to Dixie*, 20.

Chapter 9

184. Ibid., 159.
185. Angie Whitney McDonald, "Ohio Home Camp and Woodville, SC," interview by Anne Peden, June 19, 2020.
186. T.K. Peden Jr., "Florida Travelers at Moonville Service Station, 1950s," interview by Anne Peden, 1980.
187. Richardson, *History of Greenville County*, 95.
188. Huff, *Greenville*, 392–93.
189. Ingram, *Dixie Highway*, 10–11, 91–92.
190. Ibid., 85–87.

Chapter 10

191. "Below the Surface," Greenvillejournal.com, 2011.
192. Bob Dicey, "Dixie Highway on Donaldson Air Base," interview by Anne Peden, June 13, 2019. Bob Dicey, a Donaldson Air Base historian, found that there is extant concrete on the Donaldson Center. He documented where the Augusta Road crossed the base prior to its construction in 1942 and has in his collection of artifacts a military scrapbook of photos during construction with some images of where the road was being diverted. He found a small piece of the concrete across Perimeter Road from Augusta Arbor Way, which originally was Augusta Road and the Dixie Highway.
193. "South Carolina Department of Transportation." Wikipedia, March 31, 2020.
194. "Jefferson Davis Memorial Bridge," bridgehunter.com/ga/richmond/bh38525.
195. William Least Heat-Moon, *Blue Highways: A Journey into America* (New York: Little, Brown and Company, 1982), 5.

INDEX

A

African Americans 62, 71, 74, 75, 87, 108
Aiken 57, 66, 72, 98, 105, 115
Appalachian 16, 25, 40, 95
Appalachian Trail 119
Asbury, Bishop Francis 17, 36, 39, 44, 45
Asheville 23, 24, 26, 36, 38, 40, 46, 60, 68, 74, 91, 93, 97, 107, 123, 124
Atta Kulla Kulla 28
Augusta 15, 21, 25, 30, 31, 32, 33, 38, 45, 46, 50, 51, 53, 54, 55, 57, 59, 60, 64, 65, 66, 67, 69, 72, 74, 84, 90, 92, 98, 103, 105, 107, 110, 116, 129, 130, 132, 134, 140, 146, 148
Augusta Road 15, 24, 38, 42, 50, 62, 63, 64, 71, 74, 81, 82, 84, 90, 103, 112, 127, 129, 134, 136, 139, 140, 143, 146
automobile 16, 79, 80, 86, 98, 104, 116, 133, 148

B

Bankhead Highway 83, 112
Bankhead, John Hollis 83
Barnett, J. 35
Bartram, William 23, 24
Biltmore House 40
bison. *See* buffalo
Black codes 63
Boone, Daniel 31, 35
bridge 38, 68, 79, 100, 115, 119, 120, 126, 128, 133, 136, 138, 139, 144, 146, 148
Buckner, N. 102, 106
buffalo 23, 24, 27, 35
Buncombe County 32, 35, 38, 138
Buncombe Road 33, 38, 50, 64, 90, 128, 132, 138
Buncombe Turnpike 15, 32, 33, 38, 40, 54, 84, 90, 107, 116, 119, 120, 123, 124

C

Cambridge 31, 39, 50, 130

Cameron, Alexander 32
camp 45, 57, 98, 111, 127
camps 27, 33, 38, 54, 100, 111
Camp Wadsworth 98, 100
chain gang 102
Charleston 16, 27, 29, 38, 39, 40,
    53, 57, 60, 61, 64, 65, 67, 70,
    113
Charles Town 21, 25, 26, 27, 29,
    38
Cherokee 16, 24, 25, 26, 27, 28, 29,
    30, 31, 32, 33, 34, 35, 38, 50
Cherokee Path 25
Chunn family 39
Claussen-Lawrence Construction
    Company 107
Columbia 38, 59, 60, 67, 70, 73,
    90, 127
commerce 16, 29, 30, 33, 44, 61,
    65, 69, 75, 83, 85, 89, 90, 95,
    97, 98, 114, 138
concrete 16, 42, 79, 89, 90, 93,
    102, 103, 105, 107, 108, 110,
    112, 115, 119, 124, 128, 133,
    134, 135, 136, 137, 138, 139,
    140, 143, 144, 146, 148
Conestoga wagon 69, 70
construction 17, 82, 100, 102, 105,
    108, 112, 114, 115, 124, 134,
    137, 140, 142, 146
corduroy roads 67
Coronaca 50, 61, 130
cotton 17, 33, 35, 42, 47, 53, 54,
    59, 60, 61, 62, 63, 64, 65, 66,
    69, 71, 72, 74, 75, 80, 83, 84,
    85, 90, 95, 102, 140
cotton mills 59, 64, 81, 90
critter, the. *See* whiskey

D

Dark Corner 32, 95, 97, 98, 100,
    105
DeWitts Corner 34
distillation 95, 97, 98
Dixie Highway 16, 40, 42, 80, 81,
    83, 86, 89, 93, 95, 97, 98,
    100, 105, 106, 108, 109, 110,
    112, 114, 115, 132, 137, 143,
    146
Drake, Dave 63
Drayton, Governor John 37
driving clothing 93
drovers 29, 38, 50, 51, 57, 58, 59,
    71, 85, 128
drover's road 39, 40, 44, 50, 58,
    64, 65, 68, 74, 120, 124, 126,
    127, 130

E

Earle, Elias 37
Edgefield 23, 39, 50, 51, 59, 61, 64,
    67, 68, 74, 91, 98, 105, 115,
    130, 132, 143, 144, 146
education 74, 75, 109, 116, 130
Eisenhower, Dwight 110, 112, 113
enslaved 16, 26, 35, 42, 60, 61, 63,
    69, 74, 130

F

farm 44, 57, 59, 71, 82, 84, 89, 98,
    115, 126, 150
farmers. *See* farm
Fisher, Carl 86
Flat Rock 35, 42, 59, 60, 91, 124,
    126

Fletcher 115, 124, 134
food 17, 31, 50, 55, 61, 98
Fork Shoals 64, 65, 75
Fork Shoals Historical Society 47, 62, 129
Fort Charlotte 24
Fort Moore 27, 30
Franklin 35
freedmen. *See* enslaved
French and Indian War 29
French Broad River 23, 26, 35, 36, 38, 39, 40, 120
funding 17, 82, 100, 102, 103, 104

G

Good Roads Movement 79, 80, 90, 98
Goodwin House 45, 127, 137
Goudy, Robert 31
Gowan, John William 37
Gowensville 32
Graniteville 64, 66, 72, 75, 80, 90
Great Migration 87
Great Plains 32
Great Wagon Road 29
Green Book 87
Greenville 15, 24, 25, 26, 32, 34, 35, 38, 39, 40, 45, 46, 47, 59, 60, 61, 62, 65, 68, 71, 72, 73, 74, 80, 83, 90, 91, 93, 95, 97, 98, 100, 103, 105, 106, 107, 111, 115, 126, 127, 128, 129, 134, 137, 138, 139, 140, 143
Greenville Army Air Base 112
Greenwood 50, 91, 111, 130, 143, 144
Greenwood Manufacturing 74, 81
Gregg, William 66, 72

H

Hamburg 31, 51, 53, 54, 55, 57, 61, 62, 63, 64, 65, 66, 68, 69, 71, 72, 84, 90, 92, 132, 146, 148
Hammett, H.P. 72
Hampton, Wade 40
Hendersonville 42, 90, 91, 124
Hodges 91, 143
hogs 57
Hoodenpile, Philip 36
Horn's Creek Baptist Church 74
Hot Springs. *See* Warm Springs

I

Indian Territory 34
industrial small track railroad 107
inn 39, 45, 47, 50, 57, 58, 128, 137
internment camp 40

J

Jewel Hill 40, 74
Jim Crow 87

K

Kingdom of Happy Land 44, 126
Kirksey 50, 130

L

Latimer, Asbury Churchill 82, 102
Lickville 24
Lickville Presbyterian Church 74
log cabin 40
Lover's Leap 119

Lowcountry 15, 16, 29, 33, 35, 40, 42, 44, 46, 47, 59, 60, 69, 72, 110

M

maintaining. *See* maintenance
maintenance 17, 68, 69, 79, 102, 103, 107, 148
Mansion House 46, 59, 60
Marshall 40, 60, 120
McCullough, Joseph 47, 61, 159–165
Meeting Street 39, 50, 130, 166
Merrittsville 45, 127, 134, 135
military 16, 42, 100, 111, 112
Moonville 91, 111, 129, 140, 143
Mountain Park Hotel 40
mule 54, 57, 83, 84
Murray Branch Recreation Area 119

N

Nation 25, 27, 29, 32, 34, 50
National Register of Historic Places 40, 62, 148
Native Americans 16, 21, 24, 38, 39, 50
Neilson, William 36, 39
New South 91, 95, 110, 114, 116
Ninety Six 25, 26, 29, 30, 31, 32, 39, 50, 59, 61, 130
North Augusta 53, 71, 98, 105, 132

O

Ohio Home Camp 111
Old Hop 29

P

Paint Mountain 36
Paint Rock 36, 39
Palm Beach 86
Patton family 39, 40
Pearis, Richard 32
Phoenix 53, 65
Piedmont 35, 72, 81, 83, 100
Piedmont Manufacturing Company 90
Pine House 39, 51, 67, 91, 132, 146
plank road 67, 68, 71
plantation 16, 33, 42, 46, 47, 50, 54, 58, 59, 61, 63, 64, 65, 71, 72, 82, 84, 129
Poinsett Hotel 46
Poinsett, Joel 127
port 32, 38, 39, 53, 61, 64, 65, 71, 132, 148
Princeton 91, 107, 129

R

Reedy River 26, 32, 45, 46, 64, 65, 139, 140
Revolutionary War 23, 26, 29, 30, 32, 33, 34, 38, 50
ridge 26, 36, 40, 45, 46, 107, 114, 123, 140
road builders 33, 35
Rumbough, Henry 40, 60

S

Saluda 45, 60, 134, 135
Saluda Gap 15, 33, 35, 37, 38, 39, 44, 60, 68, 95, 98, 105, 127, 134

Saluda River 26, 31, 38, 45, 46, 72, 74, 83, 130, 136, 140
Savannah River 15, 24, 27, 31, 32, 38, 39, 51, 53, 64, 92, 100, 105, 108, 133, 146, 148
Savannah Town 26, 27, 30, 32, 53
Sawyer, Ben 108
settlers 23, 26, 29, 30, 32, 34, 35, 54, 55, 60, 63
Shultz, Henry 53
slave patrols 63
slaves. *See* enslaved
slave trade 26
South Carolina Canal and Railroad Company 53, 65
Spaniards 21
Spring Park Inn 128, 138
stagecoach 40, 42, 44, 45, 60
stand. *See* camp
State Road 38, 59, 60, 65, 67, 70, 112, 123, 127, 130
Stoney Point 50, 61

T

tavern 33, 39, 40, 51, 58
trade 16, 21, 26, 27, 28, 29, 30, 31, 32, 33, 35, 37, 53, 54, 55, 57, 59, 62, 64, 79, 84, 90, 116, 128, 130
traders 24, 31
Travelers Rest 45, 90, 91, 127, 128, 129, 138
Trenton 51, 64, 146
turnpike 38, 42, 60
Tuxedo 44, 45, 91, 126, 134

U

U.S. Highway 25 16, 23, 25, 46, 79, 81, 105, 114, 116, 138, 143, 144

V

valley 26, 36, 138
Vanderbilt, George 40

W

Walnut 40, 120
Walnut Presbyterian Church 74
War Between the States 33, 40, 44, 46, 71, 74, 80, 90, 97
Ware Place 47, 91, 129, 168
Ware Shoals 25, 74, 81, 91, 143
Ware, T. Ed 47
Warm Springs 15, 36, 39, 40, 58, 74, 91, 119, 120, 173
Washington District 34
whiskey 31, 55, 58
wired radio station 47
Woodside brothers 129
Woodside family 47
Woodville 47, 111, 129

Z

Zionsville 31

ABOUT THE AUTHORS

Anne Peden has always lived in southern Greenville County on property her great-grandfather purchased near the Augusta Road in 1872. An educator and avid local historian, she also has been blessed to drive trails and roads in all fifty states and several foreign countries. Anne serves on the Greenville County Historic Preservation Commission and the boards of the Fork Shoals Historical Society and the Piedmont Historic Preservation Society, and she writes National Register and State Historical Marker applications. With service clubs, she helped author two Arcadia Publishing photographic histories, *Fork Shoals* and *Piedmont.*

Jim Scott runs a productive family farm near U.S. 25 in southern Greenville County at Princeton. His businesses have allowed him to become acquainted with almost everyone in the western part of South Carolina. Jim learned local history from his grandmother and has been continuing to study and share the stories for a lifetime. He is a genealogist and historian, as well as an accomplished hunter known for training and field  trialing English pointer bird dogs. He is a director of Greenville County Farm Bureau and chairman of the Fork Shoals Historical Society.

Visit us at
www.historypress.com